LIFE IS_____.
FORTY-DAY
EXPERIENCE

A DEVOTIONAL JOURNEY
THROUGH GOD'S ILLOGICAL LOVE

JUDAH SMITH

NELSON
BOOKS

An Imprint of Thomas Nelson

Published in Nashville, Tennessee, by Nelson Books, an imprint of Thomas Nelson. Nelson Books and Thomas Nelson are registered trademarks of HarperCollins Christian Publishing, Inc.

Published in association with the literary agency of Fedd & Company, Inc., P.O. Box 341973, Austin, TX 78734.

Thomas Nelson titles may be purchased in bulk for educational, business, fund-raising, or sales promotional use. For information, please e-mail SpecialMarkets@ThomasNelson.com.

Unless otherwise noted, Scripture quotations are taken from the *Holy Bible*, New Living Translation. © 1996, 2004, 2007, 2013 by Tyndale House Foundation. Used by permission of Tyndale House Publishers, Inc., Carol Stream, Illinois 60188. All rights reserved.

Scripture quotations marked NKJV are from the New King James Version®. © 1982 by Thomas Nelson. Used by permission. All rights reserved.

Scripture quotations marked ESV are from the ESV® Bible (The Holy Bible, English Standard Version®). Copyright © 2001 by Crossway, a publishing ministry of Good News Publishers. Used by permission. All rights reserved.

Scripture quotations marked NIV are from the Holy Bible, New International Version®, NIV®. Copyright © 1973, 1978, 1984, 2011 by Biblica, Inc.® Used by permission of Zondervan. All rights reserved worldwide. www.zondervan.com. The "NIV" and "New International Version" are trademarks registered in the United States Patent and Trademark Office by Biblica, Inc.®

Library of Congress Cataloging-in-Publication Data

Smith, Judah.
  Life is -- forty-day experience : a devotional journey through God's illogical love / Judah Smith.
    pages cm
  ISBN 978-0-7180-3266-1
  1. Bible--Meditations. I. Title.
  BS491.5.S657 2015
  242'.5--dc23

                    2015010662

Printed in the United States of America

15 16 17 18 19 RRD 6 5 4 3 2 1

Contents

CONTENTS

SECTION 3: LIFE IS TO BE AT PEACE WITH GOD AND YOURSELF

SECTION 4: LIFE IS TO ENJOY GOD

CONTENTS

Introduction

Welcome to the *Life Is ____ Forty-Day Experience.* I'm excited to share the next few weeks with you! This devotional consists of forty inspirational thoughts and Bible verses. They all relate to the main concept of the *Life Is ____* book: that God is the central theme of life and that when we follow him, we find true fulfillment.

I hope these devotional thoughts and Scripture readings inspire you to live the fullest, most complete life possible. That's what God wants for you, and I believe he will show you how to do that as you learn to focus on him.

I've used a lot of real-life examples and a bit of over-the-top humor for two reasons. First, I get bored easily. I need practical and preferably entertaining things to keep me focused. Second, there is nothing more down-to-earth than God and the Bible, which is his revelation of himself to us. Spirituality was meant for the masses, not for an elite few who happen to have the willpower and moral fabric to live extra-holy lives.

If you haven't read *Life Is* _____, you might wonder why there is a blank in the title. It's because I'm not here to tell you answers. I'm not going to give you seven slick steps to success or fourteen fantastic philosophies to draw close to God. Frankly, I'm not smart enough or organized enough for that.

I'm here to point you to a person: Jesus. I'm here to show you that what you know and believe about God can give you the life you long to have. Not on just an external level— although that could happen too—but where it really matters. In your soul. In your mind, your will, your emotions, and your spiritual walk with God.

At the beginning of each devotional there is a Bible passage listed. You are welcome to read that before jumping into the devotional, or you can read it after you finish. Usually I quote some or all of it in the text.

At the end of each devotional there are several questions. You can use these however works best for you. I'd recommend writing the answers down in a journal, but you could also just answer them mentally. There are no right or wrong answers.

You are amazing, gifted, and unique. I truly believe that. And I'm not the only one—God does too. He has great things in mind for you over the next few days, or weeks, or months, or however long it takes you to read this. It would probably take me years, so no pressure.

The more you walk with God and get to know his love for you, the better life gets. So let's get started.

SECTION 1

LIFE IS TO BE LOVED AND TO LOVE

Amnesiacs

Bible Reading: Romans 8:38-39

Have you ever been tempted to use sarcasm when responding to your kids? I'm thinking in particular of confrontational situations, where you need to correct something and you'd like to inject a bit of humor. Preferably at their expense. In hindsight, that is not a good motivation.

It never works, either. At least with kids under age twelve, which is the limit of my firsthand knowledge. Usually what you say goes over their heads, and they look at you like you're from an alternate universe. The rest of the time they take what you say literally, and consequently they feel hurt—which makes you loser dad of the year.

One of the phrases that I've found myself tempted to use is this one: *What part of* no *do you not understand?* For example, we're at the store, and I've just told them for the sixty-seventh time we are not going to buy candy. I've explained the reasons why: It's unhealthy. It will torpedo their immune systems. And their mom is watching. Logical reasons. Spoken with love and patience and longsuffering.

But childhood amnesia strikes, conveniently and repeatedly. So they ask, with eyes wide in angelic and totally fraudulent innocence: "Can we buy candy, Dad? Please?"

And that's when the sarcasm tries to creep out. "What part of *no* do you not understand?"

Believe it or not, there are a few instances of divine sarcasm in the Bible, especially in the prophetic books of the Old Testament. So I feel slightly justified. But I still wouldn't recommend it as a discipline technique with literal-minded children.

Sometimes I suspect God gets just a little frustrated with our ongoing resistance. Our recurrent amnesia. Our hesitancy to believe what he has said. And if I were God, I'd probably resort to sarcasm. I'm not talking about our refusal to accept his requests and commands (although we do that sometimes too). I'm referring to the tough time we have believing the good news of the gospel and of God's love for us.

That sounds odd, I know. You would think that we would easily embrace and believe his love, and that we would wrestle against his holiness and demands. But in my experience as a pastor, most people struggle more to comprehend the love of God than the commands of God.

As humans we find it easier to believe that God wants something *from* me than believe that he wants something *for* me. We would rather believe that he has a list of complaints than that he has a list of compliments. Yet God tells us time after time—after time—that he loves us. I can't even begin to list all the verses and stories that reveal God's love.

The entire Bible is a love story. God dealt with Adam, Abraham, and Moses in love. He led Israel in love. Jesus' years on earth were a tangible demonstration of God's love. And Jesus' death and resurrection proved beyond question God's unconditional love. But we keep getting amnesia. Selective amnesia.

We remember we are sinners, but we forget we've been set free. We remember we were guilty, but we forget we've been forgiven. We remember we've fallen, but we forget that God picked us up. And I think God is up in heaven saying, "What part of *love* don't you understand?"

I want to respond, "Um, all of it?"

God's love is so drastic, so forceful, and so expansive that it really is too hard for us to grasp. But we need to try. We need to spend the rest of our lives discovering and re-discovering the simple grace of the gospel, the overwhelming and overarching love of Jesus. We need to believe it, even if we can't understand it. Paul wrote this:

> And I am convinced that nothing can ever separate us
> from God's love. Neither death nor life, neither angels nor

demons, neither our fears for today nor our worries about tomorrow—not even the powers of hell can separate us from God's love. No power in the sky above or in the earth below—indeed, nothing in all creation will ever be able to separate us from the love of God that is revealed in Christ Jesus our Lord. (Romans 8:38–39)

Note how Paul phrased it: "I am convinced." He seems to be implying that for him, believing God's love was a process and a choice. Somehow—through the Scriptures, his experiences, and his personal walk with God—he had come to the point of firmly believing God's love for him. He was convinced.

That is the journey we are on: understanding, believing, accepting, remembering, and rehearsing God's love for us.

Forget amnesia. (Oh, the irony.)

Let's be convinced of his love.

Questions for Reflection

- When is it hardest for you to remember that God loves you? Are there particular circumstances or character issues that make you forget? If so, what are they?
- Is it easier for you to accept God's love or his commands? Why?
- How convinced are you of God's love for you? What convinced you? How could you be more convinced?

2.

TMI

Bible Reading: Luke 15:11–32

There are certain things I would be happy to go my whole life without knowing. It's just too much information; too many gross details. For example: How many bacteria are exchanged when you kiss? How do toilets work? What is really in chicken nuggets?

In instances like these, ignorance may not be bliss, but at least it's less disgusting than the truth. There's one other instance where I'm happy to remain ignorant. It's with respect to the severity and gravity of my sin. I realize, mentally at least, that sin is contrary to God's nature. It's an affront to his creation and purpose. But I don't think any of us can grasp the full significance of our human depravity.

I don't mean to sound negative. Actually, the fact that we can't completely comprehend our sinfulness serves to highlight God's goodness. And that's my point. God understands everything. Even chicken nuggets. He knows the good and the bad about our lives better than we do.

And he loves us anyway.

Remember the story of the prodigal son? A son talked his dad into giving him his inheritance early, then he went and wasted it, partying with his cronies. Eventually he ended up broke and hungry, feeding pigs just to survive. One day he decided to return home and throw himself on his father's mercy. He hoped to become just a hired servant. Luke tells us how the father responded:

> So he returned home to his father. And while he was still a long way off, his father saw him coming. Filled with love and compassion, he ran to his son, embraced him, and kissed him. (Luke 15:20)

I can only imagine what the boy smelled and looked like. He had been hanging out at a pig farm, after all. Have you ever been to a pig farm? I've driven by one, and that's enough for me. The aroma itself was TMI. But his dad didn't care. He hugged him, kissed him, and brought him into his house.

That's hard for me to picture. I can't stand stains on my clothes. I can't handle the thought of germs. I can't deal with things being out of order. It's an OCD issue, and I hold my mom and older sister responsible. They trained me this way.

So if my children try to hug me but they have dirty hands

and faces, I will stiff-arm them. I don't think about it, and I can't help myself. I just do it. It's a self-defense mechanism. All I can think about when I see them is where those little hands have been, what might be on them, and what it's going to look like all over my white shirt. They are welcome to clean up, wash up, and dry off. Then—and only then—can they approach me. Sorry, kids. I'll pay for your psychiatrist someday.

My response is the polar opposite of the father of this parable, who of course represents God. God knows exactly where we've been and what's all over us. He sees the dirt and grime before we do. And he embraces us anyway. He restores us anyway.

Maybe you think you're too dirty, too filthy, too soiled for God. Maybe you think if he knew the real you, you'd never make it past the gates of his house. I've got news for you. There's no such thing as TMI with God. God knows where you've been and what you've done, and he's running down the road toward you anyway. His knowledge of your condition doesn't slow him down one bit. If anything, it makes him run faster.

He wants to embrace you. To love you. To restore you.

Questions for Reflection

- Have you ever felt ashamed of your past before God? If so, how did you process those feelings?
- How does God's unconditional love for you help you deal with any current weaknesses and flaws in your life?
- If God knows your past and loves you anyway, what does he think about your future? If you mess up down the road, how will God respond?

3.

Exaggerating Infinity

Bible Reading: Romans 8:1-2

I've discovered something about myself. I always exaggerate. I do it all the time. Life is never bland or colorless to me. I make everything bigger, crazier, and more dramatic than it actually was.

See? I just exaggerated four times in one paragraph. You can count them. Words like *always, all, never,* and *everything* are, by definition, terms of exaggeration. Those are dangerous words. Fun words, too, I might add.

This gift for verbal embellishment makes for exciting storytelling, but it doesn't always work out well in marriage. Especially since I happen to be married to a smart, literal, analytical person who actually remembers the details that I would rather lump into generalities.

So in moments of intense discussion, phrases like "But

you *always* say . . ." or "Well, you *never* do . . ." sometimes fly unplanned from my mouth. But as soon as they do, I know I've lost the argument. My poetic, hyperbole-laden speech is pointless, because the non-exaggerating half of our marriage has already mentally catalogued, outlined, and footnoted the exceptions to my sweeping statements.

Exaggeration is a great rhetorical device. But it short-circuits healthy dialogue. It can also short-circuit a healthy relationship with God—especially when it comes to dealing with our weaknesses and sins. Let me explain.

As humans, we tend to exaggerate our spiritual condition. Either we overemphasize our own righteousness or we overemphasize our sinfulness. Sometimes we do both within seconds. It's like spiritual schizophrenia.

If you're having a good day—for example, you've had minimal temptation, you've committed little to no actual sin, you kept your temper in rush hour traffic, maybe you even did a good deed or two—then you might start to think you are incredibly spiritual.

But if you lost your patience with your spouse at breakfast, yelled at the neighbor kid for leaving his bike behind the car again, and in general acted like a selfish brat during the day, you swing to the opposite extreme. You think you are a sinner who is hopelessly and irrevocably excluded from friendship with God.

The Bible calls the first exaggeration self-righteousness.

And it calls the second one condemnation. Both are wrong, and both will damage your walk with God.

Here's the best part. Humans often exaggerate—but God does not. He can't deceive, he can't lie, and he can't stretch the truth. Therefore whatever he says in the Bible is 100 percent true.

Take a look at Romans 8:1–2:

So now there is no condemnation for those who belong to Christ Jesus. And because you belong to him, the power of the life-giving Spirit has freed you from the power of sin that leads to death.

Wait. *No* condemnation? None? At all? Ever?

That sounds like an exaggeration. But it's not. It's the truth, and it has the power to set us free from our tendency to swing from self-righteousness to self-condemnation.

If we are *in Jesus*—if we trust in him for forgiveness and salvation—the guilt and condemnation of sin are a moot point. We are free to enjoy God and walk with God even though we'll stumble from time to time. Even though we'll feel guilty and ashamed from time to time.

None of us is perfect—not even close. So to think we could ever earn God's love or acceptance based on our performance would be comical if it weren't so common. We don't have to earn God's love. He already loved us before we were born. And we don't have to deserve his forgiveness. Jesus already did that once and for all.

That's the beauty of the gospel. That's why it's called "good news." It's good because anyone can receive it. It's good because it trumps our failures. It's good because it provides security even in our ups and downs.

Whether you feel angelic or diabolic at the current moment is irrelevant to your spiritual position. I don't mean to demean or undervalue your actions or emotions. Of course what you do or don't do is important. And God cares deeply about your feelings. He wants your life to be characterized by righteousness, peace, and joy. But the temporary absence of those things doesn't change your position before God.

Your position is a result of your faith, not your works. You were saved by faith, you live by faith, and someday you'll be welcomed into heaven by faith. Your good deeds and holy lifestyle are a result of your walk with God. They enhance your walk with God—but they aren't a condition for it. So don't exaggerate your goodness. And don't overemphasize your badness. Neither extreme is helping anyone.

If you are going to talk about big things, if you are going to use grand, sweeping statements—do it about God's love. Go ahead and try. Just try to exaggerate his love. To overstate his goodness. To overemphasize his faithfulness. To overestimate his kindness toward you and me.

No matter how hard you try, you won't be able to.

You can't exaggerate infinity.

Questions for Reflection

- Which extreme do you tend toward: Exaggerating your goodness or your badness? Or maybe both? Why?
- What is the relationship between your actions and emotions and your spiritual position? Explain.
- What are the biggest, broadest words you can think of to describe God's love for you? Do they do his love justice?

4.

Pet Troubles

Bible Reading: 1 John 4:8-10

I have a reaction when dogs approach me, and it's not a positive one. It usually involves flinching, screeching, and possibly climbing on available furniture.

That is my reaction if the dog is friendly and happens to be smaller than say, a cat. If I were to actually be attacked by a large and ferocious dog, the result would be catastrophic. I don't think playing dead would be an option. I would already be in heaven, a victim of sheer fright.

My reaction isn't limited to canines. It extends to anything that is hairy, scaly, slobbery, or smelly. When I see people who love their pets with a ridiculous, passionate, extravagant love, I just don't understand their sentiment. "It's an *animal*!" I want to inform these people. "It's a beast, a brute, a creature. And you are *human*. Why are you wasting your love on something so far beneath you?"

I just don't get it. How can people love dogs that shed on their sofa, soil their carpets, knock over their garbage cans, and bark all night? Why would people pay actual money for turtles and tortoises and fish and snakes and tarantulas and lizards that do nothing at all, except maybe eat other animals alive—which takes the term *disgusting* to another level?

Yet millions—perhaps billions—of people do.

Why? Not because hamsters and weasels deserve our affection. Not because mice and parakeets earn our adoration. It's because love is woven into the fabric of our nature. We love because of who *we* are, not because of who *they* are. That's how true love works. Love isn't based on the object of love, but on the source of love. Love doesn't ask, *Is this pet—or person—worthy of my love?*

We love because we are lovers, because we have love hardwired into our makeup. We love because we were made in God's image, and God is love. So if you love your rodent, reptile, canine, or feline, that's great. I applaud you. From a distance, of course.

But here's my point. In a similar but far greater way, God loves us because of who he is, not because of who we are. His love is poured out toward us because he is love. The apostle John described God's love this way:

> But anyone who does not love does not know God, for God
> is love. God showed how much he loved us by sending his
> one and only Son into the world so that we might have

eternal life through him. This is real love—not that we loved God, but that he loved us and sent his Son as a sacrifice to take away our sins. (1 John 4:8–10)

God sent Jesus to earth out of love. It was the ultimate sacrifice, and it proved beyond a doubt that God loves us just as we are. We are not worthy of God's love. We have not earned it and we never will.

And that's okay.

God isn't asking us to deserve his care and concern or to pay back his affection. He simply wants us to receive the love he generously and unconditionally offers us. That's hard to believe sometimes. We tend to think that we have to give God something in return. We assume his love for us depends—at least a little bit—on our love for him, on our holiness, and on our commitment. But it doesn't. Like cat lovers and dog lovers and pet-crazed people in general, God's love is birthed within his own heart. It comes from who he is.

That's great news for us, especially when we don't feel particularly lovable. Our emotions and dedication fluctuate, but God's love is constant. It is unending. Immovable. Forever dependable. God's love is as unchanging as he is. That means we don't have to be worried about whether he loves us today, or whether he loves us less than he did yesterday, or whether he will love us more tomorrow.

We can simply enjoy his love. We can revel and rest in the certainty that God is with us, for us, and in love with us. Knowing God loves you regardless of your performance will affect every facet of your life. It will help you face challenges, process problems, recover from failures, and enjoy victories. It will bring you freedom and peace as you've never experienced before.

Maybe you are reading this early in the morning, and you know you have a long day ahead of you. You are facing challenges and decisions, and you aren't sure you are up to the task. Or maybe you're reading it at night, and you just finished a long, tough day. Maybe things didn't quite work out how you hoped. You didn't live up to your own expectations. You don't feel very worthy of God's affection or approval.

No matter where you find yourself on the spectrum of failure and success, no matter what your emotions and thoughts might be telling you, and no matter how worthy or unworthy your life is—God's love is there for you. It overwhelms your weaknesses. It overpowers your failures. It washes you, renews you, and restores you.

Take time today to think about how great God's love is. I promise you, it will change everything.

Questions for Reflection

- Is it hard for you to believe God loves you? Why or why not?
- Do you feel worthy of God's love right now? How is that affecting your level of joy and peace?
- How would your life change if you focused more on God's love and less on your failures?

5.

Fixer-Uppers

Bible Reading: Romans 2:4

I like Disney songs. I'm just going to come out and say it. *The Lion King, Aladdin, The Little Mermaid*—those are classics. I sing them nonstop at my house, to the annoyance of my wife. Full volume. Dramatic poses. No apologies.

I realize that's not very manly. I could blame it on the fact that I have three young children. But I won't. I've been doing this for decades.

One of the most recent additions to my Disney repertoire is *Frozen*. Maybe you've seen it. At one point, a bunch of trolls—along with a snowman with a fixation on summer—sing a whole song about how we are all "fixer-uppers." The chorus ends with this line: "The only fixer-upper fixer that can fix up a fixer-upper is true, true love."

I don't get my theology from Disney. But that line actually has a lot of truth to it. Paul wrote this:

Don't you see how wonderfully kind, tolerant, and patient God is with you? Does this mean nothing to you? Can't you see that his kindness is intended to turn you from your sin? (Romans 2:4)

In other words, one of the most powerful motivators to change is recognizing how good God is, how kind he is toward us, how much he loves us.

Some of us tend to think God is all about discipline. Threats. Punishment. We know we have problems and we know he wants us to change, so we assume God is going to do whatever it takes to get our behavior and performance to line up with his holiness. We try our hardest to change, because we are afraid of God's anger. We are scared that he's counting to ten before he blows his top, and he's on eight or nine right now.

But fear and condemnation are actually terrible motivators to change. At least if we are looking for authentic, lasting change. They work great in the short term, of course. We can get ourselves to do almost anything if we feel scared enough or guilty enough.

But human beings were not meant to live under that kind of pressure permanently. God didn't design us to experience fear, guilt, shame, or threats as our status quo. If we do, eventually, we will find a way to get around the guilt, to circumvent the threat. And even worse, we will end up distancing ourselves from the one we think is imposing the pressure: God.

So when it comes to change, fear and threats backfire. Laws and rules and punishment are great at controlling us, but they are powerless to change us. God knows that. The Law of Moses wasn't meant to get people to be perfect. It was meant to get people to recognize how far from perfect they were. It wasn't a solution. It pointed people *to* the solution: Jesus.

If laws and threats can't change us, what can?

Love.

I'm not talking about romantic, emotional, feel-good love—although that's great. I'm a romantic at heart. Hence my fascination with Disney songs. I'm talking about genuine, selfless, generous love. Love that gives of itself for the benefit of another. Love that does whatever it takes to serve, protect, and heal the object of love. Love that comes from God and looks like God. That kind of love naturally produces change.

Maybe you've experienced this selfless love from a parent, a child, or a friend. You didn't feel worthy of his or her love, but it was yours anyway. And as a result, you found yourself living differently. Someone believed in you and saw you as valuable, and that simple fact made you want to live up to the person's expectations.

That's how it works with God's love and kindness. He loves us even more than those around us. He believes in us even more than we believe in ourselves. And that fact changes us.

Or at least it will to the extent we grasp his love. But often, we are too distracted with our failures and weaknesses to even think about God's love, much less explore and apply it. I'm convinced we spend too much time fixating on our failures and apologizing for our weaknesses. We invest too much effort into improving ourselves and perfecting ourselves.

Just imagine what would happen if we invested that kind of time and effort into believing God's love for us. Our entire world would change.

I'm not saying our weaknesses are unimportant. We are all fixer-uppers. But God's the fixer. He's the handyman. He's the one who repairs us. And his tool of choice is love.

Of course, we play a part in the process. That's one of the best things about being human. We get to change. We get to grow. We have a great deal of control over who we are, what we do, and who we become. But ultimately, God is the real source of our transformation and growth. His love emboldens and empowers us to become who we were meant to be.

When you catch a glimpse of his heart toward you, when you realize how passionately he backs you and believes in you, change is automatic. Growth is inevitable. Transformation takes place, not because you forced yourself to change out of fear of punishment, but because love set you free to grow in ways you never thought possible.

Take time today to let God love you. Instead of focusing on who you are not, thank God for loving who you are. And let his love transform you from the inside out.

Questions for Reflection

- Do you spend more time thinking about your failures or God's love? Why? How does that affect you?
- Why do people tend to view God as threatening and angry? Is that your view of God? Why or why not?
- What areas of your life need to improve? How can focusing on God's love help you grow in those areas?

6.

He Likes Me

Bible Reading: 1 John 4:16

I'm glad I'm no longer single. I hope that doesn't sound negative. If you are single, it's a great stage of life. I'm just happy I'm no longer in it, that's all. I no longer have to try to figure out if Chelsea likes me, or what the status of our relationship is, or whether it's too soon to say "I love you."

Not that marriage removes the guesswork, of course. For millennia, it's been the sacred and certainly impossible quest of husbands everywhere to understand their wives. But that's another topic.

If you're single, this whole business of figuring out if someone likes you is paramount. And it's a bit of a black art. It's a complex mix of trial and error, reading between the lines, asking advice from friends, and sheer guesswork.

For instance, a guy sends a girl a text message. He accidentally leaves the caps lock on because he was driving and shouldn't have been texting in the first place. So she shows it to all her friends. "He sent his message in ALL CAPS! What does that mean? Is he angry? Is he shouting? Is he just really happy?"

Emoji haven't helped much. "She used the scared face emoji. Does that mean she's excited? Or that I'm moving too fast? Or that she's thinking of breaking up with me? OMG what does it mean?"

You have to read into eye contact, body language, facial expressions, and casual comments.

"She said my hair is interesting. Is that because she loves my new haircut? Or because she just noticed it's thinning on top?"

"He gave me a side hug. Is he saying I'm like a sister to him? Or a friend? Or his soulmate?"

It's exhausting.

Romantic relationships aren't the only time we try to guess if people like us or not. Many of us do it all the time. Family, friends, neighbors, coworkers, bosses, strangers at the store—we continually wonder if we are making a good impression, if we are measuring up to people's expectations.

Some of that is normal. It's a part of being socially aware, and it's a skill that is necessary in any community. But here's the problem. Often we do the same thing with God. We think we have to read between the lines to figure out what God thinks of us. *Does he like me? Does he accept me? Does he love me?*

We analyze our feelings, we weigh our behavior, we read into our circumstances, we employ our intellect and logic—all in an effort to discover what the Bible already told us, if we would just believe it: God loves us.

We don't need to guess. We don't need to get someone else's opinion. We don't need to stay up at night wondering and worrying. It's a fact, and nothing will change that. The apostle John wrote:

> We know how much God loves us, and we have put our
> trust in his love. God is love, and all who live in love live
> in God, and God lives in them. (1 John 4:16)

No matter what happens, no matter how we feel, and no matter what circumstances we might be facing, we need to *know how much God loves us*, and we need to *put our trust in his love*.

Let me give you another illustration. My dad was one of the most secure, humble, confident people I have ever known. He could talk to anyone. He got along with everyone. Millionaires, business owners, politicians, athletes, ex-convicts, drug addicts—it didn't matter. He wasn't intimidated or insecure.

One day he told me his secret. "I just assume everyone likes me unless they tell me otherwise."

The advice probably doesn't work so well for singles. Not everyone is in love with you. But when it comes to the rest of your relationships—including your relationship with God—it is one of the most profound pieces of advice I've ever heard. I took it to heart, and I try to live by it.

With God, you don't even have to assume he likes you. He's already made clear his love for you. You just have to accept it. Accept that God likes you. Accept that he's madly in love with you. Accept that he is on your side all the time.

God will let you know if there's a problem. He'll tell you if you need to change something or fix something.

In the meantime, learn to enjoy him. Learn to love him back. Learn to know and trust in his love.

Questions for Reflection

- Do you ever doubt God's love for you? Why or why not? How should you respond when that happens?
- What does it mean to you to trust in God's love?
- How does the fact that God will let you know if you need to change something help you relax and simply enjoy him more?

7.

Emotional Kites

Bible Reading: Ephesians 3:16–19

I still believe I have to be pleased with myself to be pleasing to God. The other night that realization hit me like a 7-iron to the back of the head. Sorry for the violent imagery. I was going to say "like a ton of bricks" or "like a semitruck" but I know literally nothing about construction or truck driving. So I'll stick with what I know. Golf.

That particular evening, I was feeling anything but pleased with myself. I don't really remember why now. Emotionally and mentally, I was just not myself. That happens more than I like to admit. Maybe you can relate. After all, emotions are part of being human. Some of us are just more human than others.

For me, if something bad happens, or someone says something negative, or maybe the Seahawks lose, my emotions don't always stay as balanced as they should. I don't mean to, but suddenly I can find myself filtering life through gray and blue. Is *emotionaholic* a word? Because it pretty much describes me.

Luckily Chelsea is one of the most stable people I've ever met. So while I dip and soar all over the emotional landscape like some demented kite, she gets stuck holding the string. Anyway, that night I was trying to process whatever I was feeling, but I wasn't having much success. I was unhappy with myself. I felt inadequate, insufficient, lacking, unqualified. So I assumed God felt that way about me too.

That's a giant leap of logic, and it's dead wrong. Yet we do it all the time. Maybe we feel bad about something we did or something we didn't do. Or we are embarrassed about a character defect that we know is damaging us but never seems to go away. Or we said something that hurt someone close to us, and we hate ourselves for it.

In those moments, deep in our heads and hearts, it's easy to assume that God is as disappointed and frustrated with us as we are. We don't feel lovable or valuable or capable, so we project those feelings on God. Then we hide in shame from the one we need the most—precisely when we need him the most.

Instead of turning to God as our source for a healthy self-image, we spend our time trying to convince God that we aren't as bad as we feel we are. We apologize and repent and grovel a bit, hoping that somehow we can convince God to like us more than we like ourselves.

But as I said, that mentality is wrong. He *already* likes us more than we like ourselves. He already loves us more than we could ever deserve or imagine. Even when we aren't pleased with ourselves, we are still pleasing to God. How do I know that? Because he loved us before we loved him. He sent his Son on our behalf long before we felt worthy or even cared about being worthy.

Now we know God, and we love him, and we are growing in him. Why would he love us less now?

We need to be grounded and established in God's love. That is exactly what Paul prayed for the Ephesian church:

[I pray that God] may grant you to be strengthened with power through his Spirit in your inner being, so that Christ may dwell in your hearts through faith—that you, *being rooted and grounded in love,* may have strength to comprehend with all the saints what is the breadth and length and height and depth, and to know the love of Christ that surpasses knowledge, that you may be filled with all the fullness of God. (Ephesians 3:16–19 ESV, emphasis added)

God's opinion of us isn't rooted in our opinion of us. That line of thinking gives too much credit to our opinions and too little credit to God's incredible love. Instead, our opinion should be rooted in *his* opinion, in *his* evaluation, in *his* love.

God's love doesn't operate based on our feelings. His love is far deeper, wider, and greater than the human emotional spectrum we experience every day.

God's love is steadfast and unfailing. As one of the writers of the psalms put it: "Your unfailing love will last forever. Your faithfulness is as enduring as the heavens" (Psalm 89:2).

God's love is grounded in who he is, which means it can never fluctuate or vacillate. It is as firm as he is. As infinite as he is. As eternal as he is.

God's love doesn't rise with our successes or sink with our mistakes. It doesn't wax and wane with our moods, passions, or faith.

God doesn't evaluate our performance and measure his love out accordingly. It unequivocally and passionately surrounds us at all times.

Emotions are a normal and wonderful part of life. But they were never meant to be the barometer of God's opinion toward us. Maybe you're a kite, or maybe you're the person holding the string. Either way, God's love is the solid ground your life is based on.

And nothing can change that.

Questions for Reflection

- On a scale of 1 to 10, how emotional of a person are you? How does your emotional makeup affect your relationship with God, for both good and bad?
- When you feel unhappy with yourself, do you tend to assume God is unhappy with you? Why or why not?
- How does knowing God's unfailing love bring stability to your life?

8.

God Doesn't Do Stereotypes

Bible Reading: Psalm 139:13–14, 17–18

When a stereotypical husband comes home from a stereo-typical day at work, his wife stereotypically asks, "How was your day?" The stereotypical response is "Fine." After which the dude turns on a football game and disengages from reality until dinner is ready.

Stereotypically, anyway.

I have problems with that picture. I think I'm a manly guy, but I like to talk.

A lot.

Chelsea knows not to ask me how my day was unless she wants a full explanation, complete with dramatic reenactments and colorful words. So that stereotype calls into question my manhood. Plus, the idea that we can sum up a day in one word is ridiculous. Sorry, stereotypical man.

I have to agree with wives everywhere on that one. The details are important.

I do love football, though. I'm good with that part of the picture. But back to what I was saying about details. Humans are, by nature, detailed. We are convoluted, complex, and intricate. We are detailed by design. God made us complicated on purpose, and that's a good thing.

I'm not talking about whether or not your personality is detail oriented. That's a different topic altogether. I love details when it comes to conversation, but I'm terrible with details when it comes to, say, balancing a checkbook. Actually I don't even know what that means. Do people still do that?

I'm talking about the fact that we are a lot more complicated than we sometimes let on. And just like we can't sum up an entire day with one word—*fine*—we can't sum up our lives with one word. We can't reduce our identities to a single term or phrase. But we do it all the time.

I'm a failure.

I'm an alcoholic.

I'm a mess.

God himself doesn't even do that. Have you ever stopped to think about that? He doesn't sum us up with a single label. So why do we? David wrote this in Psalm 139:

> *You made all the delicate, inner parts of my body*
> *and knit me together in my mother's womb.*
> *Thank you for making me so wonderfully complex!*

Your workmanship is marvelous—how well I
know it . . .
How precious are your thoughts about me, O God.
They cannot be numbered!
I can't even count them;
they outnumber the grains of sand!
(verses 13–14, 17–18)

God made us "wonderfully complex." He's not intimidated by our complications. Far from it. He loves our levels and layers. He delights in our details. His thoughts toward us can't be counted, calculated, or quantified. Every piece of us, every facet of who we are and who we are becoming, is on his mind, all the time.

Here's the problem, though. Often, we pick out one detail from our lives—usually something negative, for some reason—and we make that our identity. But it's not our whole life. It's a detail. It's one facet, one component, one piece of who we are.

God's view of us is so much bigger than a single word or detail. He doesn't define us from one failure or even a string of failures. He never categorizes us based on who we are not, or what we can't do, or where we've messed up. God sees the whole picture. He understands us better than we do, and he loves us completely and profoundly.

Sometimes people think the Bible was written to tell us what to do and what not to do. That it's a rule book with a bunch of stories and poetry thrown in. That's not very accurate.

Yes, the Bible was written to show us how to live. God wouldn't be a good God if he didn't tell us how to get the most out of our lives. And avoiding sin is a giant step toward living a happy, successful life. But the Bible isn't primarily about avoiding sin. It's about knowing God and being known by him. About loving God and being loved by him. One of the greatest gifts of the Bible is that it reveals God's heart toward us. It shows us what he thinks of us, how he responds to our weaknesses, and what his plans are for us.

Jesus did that in a tangible, hands-on way when he spent three-and-a-half years walking this planet. He demonstrated how God deals with sinners. How God handles our sin and mistakes. How much God loves us, even with our complexities and our complications.

We need to stop oversimplifying ourselves. To quit underestimating the value and the beauty intrinsic to us. To avoid defining ourselves with a word or two.

Instead, we need to start listening to God's wonderful, marvelous, innumerable thoughts about us.

Questions for Reflection

- With what words or phrases do you tend to sum up your life? Are they positive or negative? Do you think God agrees with them?
- Based on what you know about Jesus and his unconditional love, what are some of the thoughts God has about you?
- Is it hard for you to believe all the good things God thinks about you? Why or why not?

9.

Idiosyncratic You

Bible Reading: Psalm 103:12–14

A friend of mine, a pastor on my staff, told me that his father-in-law had wanted to express how much he appreciated him. At the time, my friend's wife had just come out of a long period of sickness. My friend's father-in-law wanted to tell him how much he appreciated his sacrifices and the way he cared for the man's daughter.

My friend and his wife were both standing there, and with tears in his eyes, the father-in-law had said, "Thank you for loving my daughter—especially with all her idiosyncrasies."

Idiosyncrasies? The compliment was going great until he said that. What does that even mean? My friend thought it was hilarious. His wife—not so much.

Here's the deal. We all have idiosyncrasies. Quirks. Flaws. Peculiarities. We all have little things—or big things—that bug us about who we are. Maybe it's shyness. Maybe it's overconfidence. Maybe it's a lack of musical ability or athletic prowess. Maybe speaking in public terrifies us, or maybe we enjoy being the center of attention a bit too much. Maybe we have a short temper or a big mouth—or both.

Time after time, our weaknesses get us in trouble. They embarrass us. We wish we could get rid of them, but they don't seem to be going anywhere soon.

I'm convinced that God doesn't just love the good parts of our lives. He loves our weaknesses and failures as well. That sounds wrong, doesn't it? How can God love the parts of us that aren't perfect? The areas that bother us? The things we hate about ourselves?

I'm not saying he loves sin, of course. Sin isn't part of us. Sin is an intruder and a destroyer. It wasn't part of God's plan for us, and he is committed to helping us overcome it. But not every weakness is sin. Not every flaw is an intruder. And not every idiosyncrasy is going to go away.

And God's okay with that. He loves us just as we are. David wrote this:

> *[God] has removed our sins as far from us*
>   *as the east is from the west.*
> *The LORD is like a father to his children,*
>   *tender and compassionate to those who fear him.*
> *For he knows how weak we are;*
>   *he remembers we are only dust.*
>   (Psalm 103:12–14)

Notice that God removes our sins. He forgives them, he forgets them, and he helps us live free from them. But he doesn't necessarily remove our weaknesses. This psalm says he knows them and he takes them into account—but it doesn't say he always fixes them.

That's an important distinction, because sometimes we think that God doesn't like us because we have weaknesses. Because we have tendencies toward sin. Because we still struggle with temptation, and we often lose the fight. Sometimes we think that God would love us more if we were better people. So we focus on what is lacking and obsess over what is missing. We are convinced that if we can just improve a bit, we will convince God to accept us more.

I've got news for you. He already accepts you as much as he will ever accept you. He already loves you as much as he will ever love you. Maybe, just maybe, you need to accept and love *yourself.* Maybe you need to learn to listen to what God is saying about you, and then let that trump your thoughts, your emotions, and your judgments about yourself.

What if the things that bug you are the things that God loves the most? What if he has plans to use precisely those things to accomplish his purposes through you? Sure, he'll probably transform many of your weaknesses over time. But I don't think he's in as big a hurry to change you as you are.

God loves *all* of you. Even your idiosyncrasies.

Questions for Reflection

- What are some of your weaknesses or idiosyncrasies that bother you?
- Do you think God wants to fix those weaknesses eventually? Explain your answer.
- How does the fact that God loves all of you, even your quirks and flaws, help you accept those things and deal with them?

10

Loving Failure

Bible Reading: John 21:1-25

One of the supposed keys to success in sports is not to get too emotional over your failures. When you make a mistake or lose, you shouldn't take it personally or let it affect your attitude. Learn from your failure and move on.

That is the theory, anyway. And one of these days, I intend to try it. But in the meantime, I am human. And emotional. So when I hit a golf ball into a water hazard for the third time in a row, it's hard for me to be philosophical about it. And I have a collection of bent and broken golf clubs to prove it.

Actually, I don't fully agree with the no-emotion idea. I think it's impossible to throw your heart and soul and body into an activity without being emotionally invested in the outcome. But being emotional about your failure is not the same thing as being stuck in your failure. Or defining yourself by your failure. Or reliving and rehearing ad infinitum your failure.

It's bad enough to have to retrieve golf clubs from trees and lakes because your emotions got the best of you. But it's even worse to let those emotions continue to dominate you during the rest of the game. That, in my mind, is the real failure. When failure gets in your head, it tends to propagate itself. You start to think about how badly you are failing, which makes you fail more. And that makes you feel like more of a failure, which consequently leads to further failure.

It's a nasty cycle. And it's a selfish one too—because all you think about is how badly you did, how embarrassed you feel, and how hopeless you are. So what do failures and golf temper tantrums have to do with God? A lot.

When it comes to following Jesus, failure is not only an option, it's a fact of life. It's inevitable. I don't mean to be pessimistic, but think about it for a second. God is perfect. Jesus is perfect. The bar is impossibly high.

That means we better have a game plan for failure, or we are going to spend our entire lives dealing with guilt and condemnation. And like the failure cycle I mentioned a moment ago, guilt tends to propagate itself. The worse we feel about ourselves, the worse we behave—and the worse we feel.

We only have a record of one disciple being there when Jesus was dying on the cross. His name was John. The Bible doesn't specify where the others were, but we do know that just prior to Jesus' capture, they had all fled. So it's probable they were in hiding.

Peter was especially vocal in disassociating himself from Jesus. The Bible records three different moments when he denied having followed or known Jesus. This was the same Peter who had walked on water—more or less—and who had correctly identified Jesus as the Messiah, the Son of God. He appears to have been the leader of the disciples. Earlier, he had promised to never abandon Jesus. Yet when it counted the most, he turned his back on him.

That takes failure to a whole new level.

Meanwhile, John had also denied Jesus and fled. But he came back. Within hours, he had figured out how to process his failure and move on. And when Jesus needed someone to watch out for his mother, John was there.

I think the clue to what helped John break the cycle of guilt and failure while Peter ended up crying in shame is found in their relationship to Jesus. Peter was a leader. He was a talker. He was a doer. He was brash and brave and strong. But John understood Jesus' love.

In particular, John understood how to *receive* Jesus' love. He called himself "the disciple that Jesus loved" five different times in the gospel he wrote. John literally identified himself by the fact Jesus loved him. That was how he saw himself. It was his title and his identity. Jesus' love was more real to him than his own strengths, weaknesses, accomplishments, or failures.

I'm not saying Peter didn't believe Jesus loved him. But there was something unique about John. Something that enabled him to bounce back after the most colossal, humiliating blunder of his lifetime. Something that motivated him to rush back to the feet of the one he had just failed, despite the derision and the danger that entailed.

It was love. First his belief in Jesus' love for him, and second his own love for Jesus. Love overcomes fear, guilt, and failure. Love looks beyond itself and thus is immune to the cycle of failure.

When Jesus rose from the dead, he found Peter, John, and the others fishing. Jesus seemed intent on helping Peter find restoration. But he didn't tell Peter to try harder. He didn't ask him to fast and pray. He didn't question him about his thought life. He asked him about his love. "Simon, son of John, do you love me?" (John 21:15, 16, 17).

Just like a few missed putts make me think I'm a lousy golfer, a few sins can make me think I'm a lousy Christian. I can start to look at myself as a failure, a loser, someone who can never please God. But that's wrong.

My identity can't be wrapped up in my performance. It must be wrapped up in Jesus' love. The fact that Jesus loves me and I love him back enables me to break the cycle of guilt and failure.

Next time you find yourself frustrated with failure, don't let it define you or sideline you. Focus on Jesus' love.

Then get back in the game.

Questions for Reflection

- How do you tend to react to failure? Is it hard for you to forget about the past and move on?
- How would living in regret and shame and guilt affect your life?
- How does focusing on Jesus' love help you break the cycle of guilt and failure?

SECTION 2

LIFE IS TO TRUST GOD IN EVERY MOMENT

SECTION 4

USERS TO TRUST GOD IN EVERY MOMENT

Feed Me

Bible Reading: Hebrews 13:8-9

One of the defining characteristics of kids is their tendency to change their minds without warning or reason. Yesterday one child ate cereal for breakfast, lunch, and dinner; today he won't touch it. Last week another child wore nothing but pink; now she says pink is a little girl's color and she'll never wear it again.

But there is a particular stage, somewhere around two or three years old, where this tendency to change their minds is more than a cute little quirk. It is their obsession. Their occupation. Their default. During this stage, every single conversation goes something like this:

"Dad, I hungry. Feeeeed meeeeeee."

"Sure, do you want a banana or a piece of toast?"

"I wanna cookie."

"No, you can have a banana or toast. Pick one. Only one. Nothing else but one of those. Please choose now."

"Banana."

So you peel a banana and hand it to him.

"I want toast!"

"You said banana."

"Toast!"

"Okay, fine. Here's some toast."

"No, I wanna banana!"

"Are we really still having this conversation? Here, take both."

"No, I wanna cookie!"

That's the abbreviated version. The real conversation would have included complaints about the fact you peeled the banana instead of letting him do it, what flavor of jam you put on the toast, the color of the plate, and so on.

This inability to make a decision that lasts longer than .08 seconds must coincide with some developmental stage of their psyche and their will. Or maybe it's cosmic revenge for our own childhood rebellion. Supposedly as we grow up, our tastes stabilize a bit. And we get better at making choices and living with the consequences. But we never outgrow growth. We never arrive at some state of perfection or nirvana where change becomes unnecessary.

God, on the other hand, does not change. He doesn't improve or grow or stabilize because he's already perfect. The author to the Hebrews said this about Jesus:

Jesus Christ is the same yesterday, today, and forever. So do not be attracted by strange, new ideas. Your strength comes from God's grace, not from rules about food, which don't help those who follow them. (Hebrews 13:8–9)

You've probably read the first verse. But the second verse provides an interesting context. The writer is talking about our walk with God. We have been saved by grace through Jesus. Because Jesus doesn't change, we don't have to worry that our salvation and standing before God are going to change. We don't need to get distracted by other doctrines and new rules that supposedly make us more righteous. Jesus already made us righteous, and that isn't going away.

As humans—even adult humans—we have a tendency to change our minds. Not about our midmorning snacks, but about grace. About our acceptance by God. About our righteousness.

We look at our mistakes and our weaknesses, and we start to think that maybe God is mad at us after all. We get distracted from grace, and we wonder if maybe our performance and our rules are the keys to pleasing God. I don't mean to impose my parental problems on God, but I wonder if our conversations with him are similar to those of a two-year-old at times.

"Do you want grace or rules?"

"Grace. No, I mean rules. No, actually grace!"

"Really? Are we still having this conversation?"

Of course rules have their place. Our actions and behavior are important. We all know that. But the source of our righteousness is far more stable, permanent, and trustworthy than our fickle performance or rule keeping.

We are secure because of the unchangeableness of Jesus.

Questions for Reflection

- Do you ever find yourself slipping into old habits of trying to be accepted by God based on your actions? What is wrong with that?
- How does the fact that Jesus never changes help you trust him?
- What are five things about Jesus that you are glad never change?

12.

Revenge of the Kitchen Appliances

Bible Reading: Psalm 91

The other night I was up late. It was dark and quiet and the kids were in bed, which is really the only time it is ever quiet in our house. Chelsea was doing something. I don't remember what, but I'm sure it was productive. I was doing something equally as productive—like watching Sports Center.

Suddenly, the serenity of the scene was shattered by a horrendous noise. It came from the kitchen—a crashing, banging, grinding, awful sound that echoed through the night and scared me beyond reason. I think I screamed at a pitch typically reserved for junior high girls. I charged bravely into the kitchen, fully prepared to defend my castle against some marauding monster. Or maybe I peeked timidly around the corner. For some reason my memory fails me.

No one was there.

Just the refrigerator, blinking in the night, and other normal kitchen appliances. When my heart slowed down enough to think, I realized what it was. The icemaker.

I had just about lost my sanity and salvation and bladder control because the icemaker chose that moment to do its thing. It was anticlimactic, to say the least. Slightly embarrassed by my overreaction, I returned to my spot on the couch and tried to breathe normally.

I wish I could say that was the only time that happened, but honestly, that dumb machine has freaked me out more times than I care to admit. It has a sneaky way of interrupting my peace and tranquility right when I least expect it. I'm convinced the manufacturer, out of some sadistic sense of humor, programmed the beast to be triggered by silence.

On a spiritual level, we can experience something similar. Things can be calm. Peaceful. Still. Then suddenly, out of nowhere, chaos breaks out. Bad news starts clanging and crashing. Maybe a plan we had at work falls through. Or someone in our family becomes seriously ill. Or the economy hits a speed bump and our investments are at risk.

In an instant, we can go from peace to panic. From rest to distress. Adrenaline kicks in. Concerns crowd our thoughts. We start to worry about what has happened and what might happen next.

Much of the time, our stress is due to our uncertainty. We don't know what's around the corner, so we fear the worst.

But often, just like the icemaker, the things that startle us into panic aren't real dangers at all. They are just the noises and confusion of life. They sound threatening. They freak us out because we didn't see them coming and we don't know what they are. But in the end, they are just noise.

Please don't get me wrong. I don't mean to minimize tragedies or genuine threats. I know there are times in life when we go through real loss and grief. But those are the exceptions. Much of the time, our fear and alarm are based on vague, scary-sounding things that haven't materialized and likely never will.

God didn't design us to be jumpy. To be nervous. To always be on our guard. He designed us to trust him, even when life gets chaotic or frightening. Psalm 91 is one of the best passages in the Bible on trusting God in the face of fear. It says:

> *Those who live in the shelter of the Most High*
> *will find rest in the shadow of the Almighty.*
> *This I declare about the LORD:*
> *He alone is my refuge, my place of safety;*
> *he is my God, and I trust him . . .*
> *Do not be afraid of the terrors of the night,*
> *nor the arrow that flies in the day.*
> (Psalm 91:1–2, 5)

This passage says the secret to living free from fear is the presence of God. It's *living* with God. Not just running to him when we have trouble or visiting him on the weekends, but making his presence our permanent home. True rest is found in God. His presence dispels panic and produces peace.

By the way, trust doesn't mean we become stoic, emotionless androids who are never affected by anything. When life scares us out of our wits from time to time, it's only natural to jump up and look for danger. But the point is that we can't *live* that way. Always looking over our shoulders. Always dreading the future. Always overreacting to potential danger.

Fear works because of the element of surprise. It affects us because we don't have full knowledge of and control over what is happening. We hear a noise and assume the worst. We feel alone, and we don't know if we will be able to fend off the danger, so panic takes hold. But God isn't limited as we are. Nothing is unexpected for him. Nothing is too dangerous or too powerful for him.

We don't know the future, but we don't need to—we know the God who knows the future. And it holds no fear for him. God knows exactly what is going on, and he wants to give us his confidence. He wants to assure us that we are not alone. He is watching out for us, and the future is under control.

We need to live in the shadow of God's strength. We need to dwell in the shelter of his goodness and greatness.

That is where true life is found.

Questions for Reflection

- Do you tend to worry easily? Why or why not?
- How does believing that God knows the future help you trust him even in uncertain circumstances?
- What are some practical ways to experience God's presence in your life?

13

Jesus Is Beast Mode

Bible Reading: John 11:1-44

Seattle sports fans—also known as the 12th man—are legendary. We are renowned around the sports world and probably the universe as the loudest, most loyal fan base to ever support any team in the history of organized sports. I may or may not be slightly prejudiced. But I know of no other group of fans whose cheers have registered on the Richter scale.

True story.

It's called the Beast Quake, and it happened in 2011 when Marshawn Lynch plowed through a ridiculous amount of defenders for a game-winning 67-yard touchdown in a wildcard playoff game. Lynch's almost superhuman ability to break tackles and penetrate defenses has earned him the nickname Beast Mode.

Speaking of sports fans, we are odd creatures. I say *we*

because I is one. Guilty as charged. Watching sports is my addiction and I'm in no hurry to get free.

When our home teams are doing poorly, we criticize them. We mock them. We armchair-manage them. We still love them, of course, but it's sort of a tough love. It could easily be confused with hatred. But let there be one glimmer of hope that our team might possibly, by some miracle, perchance, make it anywhere near the playoffs, and instantly hope comes alive. We dig out our team gear. We paint our faces. We scream and yell. We act like we never doubted.

There's a story in John 11 about another case of buried dreams and revived hope. It's the story of Lazarus's death and resurrection. In case you haven't read it, Lazarus and his sisters Mary and Martha were some of Jesus' best friends. One day Jesus got word that Lazarus had become very ill. A short time later, he died.

Jesus traveled to their home. Martha was waiting for him. She told him if he had been there, Lazarus might not have died. Jesus didn't argue with that. He simply said, "Your brother will rise again" (verse 23).

Martha responded, "Yes, he will rise when everyone else rises, at the last day" (verse 24).

But that wasn't what Jesus meant. He intended to do a miracle then and there. He planned to give Martha what she didn't dare ask or even hope for but wanted more than anything.

I'm not surprised Martha reacted with a bit of resignation. Death is, by definition, final. It's the end of life. It's the end of dreams. Martha's hopes had been dashed and her expectations had been buried. Lazarus was dead, and that wasn't going to change until "the last day," which referred to heaven.

She had resigned herself to reality. But Jesus was about to redefine her reality. He said to her:

> "I am the resurrection and the life. Anyone who believes in me will live, even after dying. Everyone who lives in me and believes in me will never ever die. Do you believe this, Martha?"
>
> "Yes, Lord," she told him. "I have always believed you are the Messiah, the Son of God, the one who has come into the world from God." (verses 25–27)

I love Martha's faith here. Not because it's so strong—far from it. She doesn't seem ready to believe that Lazarus could miraculously come back to life. But she believed in Jesus. And that was enough.

Sometimes we don't know what to ask for or hope for. Our dreams have been destroyed and our hopes are languishing in the grave. We don't know what to believe for or where to leverage our faith. That's okay.

We can get so wrapped up in how weak or how strong our faith is that we end up focusing more on our faith than on Jesus. But that's backward. Jesus is the source of our miracle. He is hope personified.

Martha had hope, not because things around her

had changed, but because she turned her focus from her impossible circumstances to her unstoppable Savior.

Sure, Marshawn Lynch is impressive. He can run, dodge, push, stiff-arm, and generally intimidate his way through impossible situations. It takes a lot to take him down. But that's nothing compared to Jesus. Jesus can't be stopped. He can't be taken down by anyone or anything.

After Jesus talked to Martha, he proceeded to Lazarus's tomb. Then he raised him from the dead. And probably fist-bumped him as he walked out. And like Lynch, probably refused to speak to the media afterward.

Maybe your dreams have been delayed, damaged, or even destroyed. Maybe failures or sins or circumstances have stopped you.

Jesus is your source of hope. He is the miracle you need. Jesus is Beast Mode.

Questions for Reflection

- Do you have any dreams that you have buried because of failure or difficult circumstances? Is there still hope? Why or why not?
- How is having faith in Jesus different from having faith in faith?
- How does knowing that Jesus is unstoppable help you face impossible circumstances?

14

Cops and Robbers

Bible Reading: Romans 8:31-39

Imagine you are walking through an area of town you don't recognize. It's late, you are alone and nervous, and you are starting to wonder if you are lost. This is a bit cliché, I know—but go with me for a moment on this. You might as well imagine dramatic, suspenseful music in the background while you're at it. And rats. There are always rats rustling in the weeds.

You find yourself in a narrow alley between sketchy-looking buildings. There are no streetlights, and dark shadows dominate the abandoned streetscape. You are getting more creeped out by the second. Then you hear footsteps ahead. Suddenly a huge figure lurches around the corner and into view. You can't tell who he is because it's too dark and he's silhouetted by lights in the distance. But you can see something outlined on his hip and it looks like a holster.

Then he sees you. There's no doubt about it. Now he's coming toward you. On purpose. And fast. Thirty seconds ago you were alone, and you wanted company. Now someone is about to join you. But there is nothing reassuring about it at all. It's downright terrifying, actually. You're about to lose control of your emotions and possibly some bodily functions.

Now imagine that the figure calls out, "Sir? Ma'am? Can I help? I'm a policeman. Are you okay?"

With those simple words, what would happen in your mind and emotions? Instantly, fear would be replaced by security. Your instinct to run from the person would be replaced by an instinct to run toward him. And maybe hug him and sob on his shoulder for a moment.

We're assuming, of course, that you aren't currently running from the law. That would be a completely different set of emotions. Just thought I'd throw that out there.

What changed? Not the size of the stranger, or the gun on his hip, or the fact that you've never met him. That all remains the same. What changed was *your perception of his intent*. Before, you feared the worst. You thought he might be against you. You assumed he was a threat. But now you know he is on your side. He is there to help and defend and protect.

The Bible reveals time after time that God is both *with* us and *for* us. Both of those are important. If we just assume that God is with us but not for us, we will tend to get a little freaked out by him. He's huge, after all. And he carries more than just a gun. He has all the power in the universe. So if he is against us, if he is a threat to us, then his power isn't reassuring at all. It's terrifying. Petrifying. Paralyzing.

Sometimes our perception of God's intent is wrong. We know he is with us, but we aren't so sure he is for us. He might be a threat. He might even be against us. We don't say that, of course. We try to believe he loves us. And most of the time, we do. But sometimes doubts creep in. Especially when we feel alone and lost or when circumstances aren't going the way we wish. In those moments, God can feel like our enemy.

Even worse, we often *do* feel like we are running from the law. We've done some things we aren't proud of. Maybe God is the last person we expect to help us. We are the robbers, and he is the cosmic cop.

Here's the deal. We all used to be crooks. Criminals. But we aren't anymore. Jesus took care of that on the cross. Our rap sheet went through the shredder. Our fingerprints were deleted from the system. There is no record of our mistakes anywhere. We are fine, upstanding citizens now.

That means that protection and assistance aren't just a vague hope. They are our rights as citizens. We can expect God to help. We can believe for and depend on his intervention because he is on our side. The Bible states this clearly in the book of Romans:

What shall we say about such wonderful things as these? If God is for us, who can ever be against us? Since he did not spare even his own Son but gave him up for us all, won't he also give us everything else? Who dares accuse us whom God has chosen for his own? No one— for God himself has given us right standing with himself. (Romans 8:31–33)

Often when we talk about God's infiniteness and omnipotence, we do so in reference to his holiness. He is big and he is perfect, so we should be awestruck. Reverent. And definitely well behaved.

That's true—but it's only part of the picture. I think we should spend a lot more time pondering how his infinite greatness applies to his goodness. How his incredible power assures our protection. How his unchallenged dominance guarantees our deliverance.

Think about how big God is. Now imagine the entire weight of that bigness fully engaged in loving you. Entirely committed to doing you good all your life. Completely devoted to surrounding you and sweeping you up in his embrace.

How awesome is that? The most powerful being in the universe accompanies you and defends you. His presence and his protection are unstoppable, irresistible, and inevitable.

God is with you. And God is for you.

What more do you need?

Questions for Reflection

- Why is it important to understand not only that God is with you but also that God is for you?
- Is it hard for you to believe that God is for you? Why or why not?
- How does knowing that God's intent toward you is to protect and bless you help you face uncertainties and threats?

15.

When Sharks Fly

Bible Reading: Mark 4:35-41

There is something about storms that is exhilarating and inspiring. At least when you are on solid ground. If you happen to be in a jet hurtling through them, it's mostly just terrifying. Jets and storms shouldn't go together.

Actually, I can think of a combination even worse than that: *boats* and storms. That doesn't appeal to me on any level. The open ocean, tidal waves, and being trapped in a giant floating box—not my idea of a relaxing vacation.

Our culture seems to be fascinated by the thought of storms at sea, though. Just look at the silver screen. For example, there was the ill-fated boat *Andrea Gail* in the movie *The Perfect Storm*. Tom Hanks and his creepy volleyball in *Castaway*. And don't forget the most classic storm scene of all: *Gilligan's Island*.

More recently, we have *Sharknado*. That's a cross between *shark* and *tornado*, in case you were wondering. The movie revolves around the highly realistic plotline of a series of twisters that suck thousands of Great White sharks up from the ocean and hurl them strategically around the LA area. The sharks only have one thing on their minds, and it's not wondering why they are falling from the stratosphere, as you might think.

It's eating people.

Even more unbelievable than that, the filmmakers found funding and an audience to make *Sharknado 2*, and rumors are flying—no pun intended—that more movies could be on the horizon.

Yes, something is wrong with the universe.

I think our fascination with storms comes from the fact that they are so much bigger than we are. They are out of our control. In the face of these storms, humans are puny and powerless.

The Bible mentions a number of storms, actually. One of the most famous ones occurs in Mark 4. No sharks are mentioned, but if Hollywood ever makes this into a movie, someone will undoubtedly write them into the script.

Jesus and his disciples were crossing the Sea of Galilee. Jesus was asleep on a pillow in the back of the boat. Then a storm began. But this wasn't your average storm. The Bible calls it a "great windstorm," and it must have been ridiculous because these seasoned, experienced fishermen started freaking out. The waves were enormous, water was filling the boat, and they were panicking.

So they woke up Jesus. "Teacher, don't you care that we're going to drown?" (verse 38). I love their choice of language. "Don't you care?" You can hear the frustration in their voices. They were about to die, and Jesus wasn't helping them. He wasn't concerned. He wasn't even awake.

They concluded, *he doesn't care*.

Jesus woke up. He yawned. He stretched. Mark wrote:

He rebuked the wind and said to the waves, "Silence! Be still!" Suddenly the wind stopped, and there was a great calm. Then he asked them, "Why are you afraid? Do you still have no faith?" (verses 39–40)

And then he probably finished his nap.

Now the disciples were more freaked out than ever. Five minutes earlier they were scared of a storm because it was so much bigger and stronger than they were. But asleep in their boat was someone bigger and stronger than even the storm.

Jesus wasn't mocking them by sleeping. He wasn't making light of their danger or their fear. He was preaching a sermon to them from his pillow. And he was preaching to us as well.

The disciples were in awe of someone who could calm storms. But they should have been in awe of someone who could *sleep through* storms. Jesus' physical posture didn't mean he didn't care. It meant he had everything under control. The very fact that Jesus could snore through their storm should have given the disciples a clue that they weren't going down. They weren't going to drown.

Now, if Jesus would have been sweating and screaming and frantically inflating a lifeboat—that would have been cause for worry. If God ever gets nervous, we should be terrified. But if he's asleep, then things are going to work out just fine. Guaranteed.

I don't know about you, but I am a lot like these disciples. Life gets rough, circumstances get choppy, and I get frightened. Jesus doesn't seem to be too concerned about my situation, so I assume he doesn't care. But he does, of course. It's just that he already has things figured out. He saw the storm coming long ago. And he already sees what is beyond the storm. He sees the other side of the lake and the great things that are in store.

Jesus had work to do on the other side. There were people with needs. People who were hungry for God, and Jesus had the answer. So right now, he needed rest. Why should he waste energy and sleep on a storm?

Jesus doesn't want us to live a lifestyle of panic. Of being awed by storms. Of struggling to survive. He wants us to learn to rest in him. To rest like him. To laugh at storms and waves and voracious, airborne, man-eating sharks.

The storm is bigger than us, but God is bigger than the

storm. So God invites us to look beyond the storm and save our resources for the opportunities and needs that will come our way.

Storms come and go, but Jesus is always with us.

His presence is our guarantee of safety.

And once the storm blows past, we will discover great things on the other side.

Questions for Reflection

- Have you ever felt like God didn't care about a situation you were going through? In retrospect, how can you see God's hand at work during your storm?
- Are you going through any storms right now? What are they? Are you able to trust God right now, or it is a struggle?
- How does knowing that God is not scared by your storms help your attitude and thoughts?

16.

Superhero Status

Bible Reading: Hebrews 7:18–28

I'm currently in my midthirties. Actually my upper-midthirties. The lower end of my upper-midthirties, to be precise. But I'm sliding down the other side faster than I'd like.

Thirty-ish years ago, when I was a kid, we played with action figures. They were basically the boy version of dolls, but if you called them that you'd have gotten a black eye. People weren't quite as politically correct back then.

Transformers, GI Joes, X-Men—those were real toys. Those were classics. Most of those action figures had cartoons that went with them. Plus there were comic books about legendary figures like Superman, Batman, and Spiderman. We were surrounded and enthralled and entertained by fantastic heroes with superhuman powers.

My generation has grown up. Or we've grown up as

much as we ever will, anyway. And Hollywood has noticed. Approximately every twenty-eight seconds, Hollywood produces another superhero movie featuring one of our childhood heroes. They know every last one of us will go watch those movies because we want to relive our glorious childhood fantasies.

And it works. So they keep doing it. Now toymakers are producing new dolls—er, action figures—based on these movies, which we buy for our kids when our wives aren't with us. And thirty-ish years from now, the next generation of kids will watch the next generation of movies based on those action figures.

It's the cycle of life. And someone is making a lot of money off of it.

What is it about superheroes that captures our attention and sparks our imaginations? Why do we have this fascination and infatuation with biologically enhanced, radiation-mutated, alien-modified beings?

I think it's the idea of hope. A hope in something beyond ourselves, better than ourselves, bigger than ourselves. Superheroes remind us that even in the most dismal, dire circumstances, there is always hope. Hope is one of the greatest characteristics of mankind.

The very fact that humanity can hope gives me hope that there is hope for humanity.

That was profound, even though I'm not sure it made sense.

Here's my point. It's not in our nature to give up. Even when hope has been dashed and trampled on and pummeled time after time, it never seems to completely die. We instinctively look for miracles. Deep inside, we believe that someone, somewhere, somehow might save us. We are not alone against the universe. I think Hollywood knows that better than Jesus-followers sometimes. We need to learn to live with hope, because of all people, we know the source of hope.

We looked at Romans 15:13 earlier: "I pray that God, the source of hope, will fill you completely with joy and peace because you trust in him. Then you will overflow with confident hope through the power of the Holy Spirit."

Hope originates with God. He is our source of hope, he is the God of hope, and he is the object of our hope. Hope is his gift to us.

The biggest obstacle mankind faces is not asteroids or zombie invasions, of course. It is sin. It is the separation between God and man that comes from sin. And we need a superhero to come to our rescue.

Thousands of years before Jesus, God gave Israel the Law. He gave them the Ten Commandments and a laundry list of other requirements to deal with sin.

But the point of the Law was not that we could save ourselves. It was the exact opposite. The Law illustrated the *impossibility* of saving ourselves. That's why God instituted such an intricate system of sacrifices—to make up for human failures in keeping the Law. The Law couldn't save us. It wasn't the hero or the savior humanity was looking for. But it did point to the one who could save us: Jesus.

The book of Hebrews spends a lot of time on this subject. It describes how Jesus came to do what laws written on stone tablets and animal sacrifices could not do. It tells us that we can now draw close to God in confidence because of the sacrifice of Jesus. Hebrews, chapter 7, says this:

> Yes, the old requirement about the priesthood was set aside because it was weak and useless. For the law never made anything perfect. But now we have confidence in a better hope, through which we draw near to God. (verses 18–19)

If we aren't careful, we can end up treating our rules and rituals like superheroes. We think they are the answer for our sins and our weaknesses. So we try harder, pray harder, and work harder. We pile on more rules and make more sacrifices.

It makes us feel spiritual—for a short time, anyway. But it never works. Even if by sheer willpower we succeed in improving our performance, we are no closer to saving ourselves than before.

Our hope rests solidly on Jesus. He is our "better hope." He is our source of confidence. Jesus is better than our best efforts. He's better than our biggest accomplishments. He's better than religion, better than rules, and better than self-improvement. When we put our trust in him, sin has no power over us.

Maybe no one has made him into an action figure yet, but the fact remains: Jesus is our superhero.

Questions for Reflection

- How would you define hope?
- Do you think mankind's biggest obstacle is sin? Why or why not?
- How does Jesus offer us hope in the battle against sin? What does it mean to have confidence in Jesus as our "better hope"?

17.

Math Fail

Bible Reading: 1 Corinthians 1:18–31

I'm fairly certain, after intense biblical research, that math is from the devil. Or if it is from God, it was never part of his original creation and instead was inflicted upon mankind as a result of sin. That makes sense to me. Adam was cursed with hard, painful work. Eve was cursed with hard, painful childbirth. And students everywhere were cursed with hard, painful calculations involving trains and velocities and pie. Er, *pi*. As in π.

Actually I liked *pi*. Not because I ever knew the concept behind it or even the number it stood for, but because it was fun to draw.

I ended up flunking pre-algebra. Twice. So my mom hired a tutor, a family friend I called Aunt Barb, and eventually we passed. I say "we" because it was a team effort. Aunt

Barb and my mom should get honorary mention on my high school diploma.

My analytical skills might be lacking, but I have good visual memory. So by the third time through pre-algebra, I could remember the answers to the tests. I didn't know much about the steps involved, but I knew the answers. Between Aunt Barb's tutoring and recalling test answers, I ended up with straight As. True story.

I'm not advocating memorizing answers without understanding the process. We have brains for a reason. God gave us the ability to think, analyze, reason, and solve. But in my case, I had to trust the answer even though it didn't make sense. I had to accept that the end result was true even though I couldn't wrap my brain around all the theories and variables and formulas.

Sometimes life can be like that. As Jesus-followers, we know the answer to the questions of life—ultimately, everything comes back to Jesus. Life is about knowing Jesus, trusting in Jesus, loving Jesus, and following Jesus.

But no matter how hard we try, there are some things in life that we won't be able to figure out. And I'm not talking about polynomials and quadratic equations. I'm talking about life circumstances that just don't make sense. About tragedies and threats and loss that blindside us. Sometimes, life doesn't make sense. Sometimes, all we have is the answer.

And that's okay.

Paul understood this concept. He wrote about it to the Corinthian church:

> Remember, dear brothers and sisters, that few of you were wise in the world's eyes or powerful or wealthy when God called you. Instead, God chose things the world considers foolish in order to shame those who think they are wise. And he chose things that are powerless to shame those who are powerful . . . God has united you with Christ Jesus. For our benefit God made him to be wisdom itself. Christ made us right with God; he made us pure and holy, and he freed us from sin. (1 Corinthians 1:26–27, 30)

In other words, following Jesus isn't about head knowledge. It isn't about figuring everything out. It isn't about being smart enough to debate our way into heaven. It's about Jesus. It's about being united with Christ. Jesus is the answer even when we don't understand the process we are going through.

I think those of us who are algebra challenged might even have an advantage here because we are used to not being able to figure everything out. Accepting answers on faith is how we survived high school math.

Please don't get me wrong. I don't think following Jesus is illogical. I'm not saying for a second that you have to turn off your brain to accept God. I think Christianity is the most logical path, because for me it explains the intricacies and the mysteries of life better than any other religion or worldview out there.

We are finite beings. We have a limited perspective of life. There will be things about life that just don't make sense, at least for now. But we have the answer. He's a person, and his name is Jesus. If we follow him and trust him, sooner or later, the pieces will fall into place. The things that confuse us and cause us to doubt won't seem so mysterious. They might even be the very things that build our future.

Jesus makes life make sense.

Sometimes that's all you need to know.

Questions for Reflection

- In what ways does logic enhance your walk with God? In what ways can logic get in the way if you don't understand trust?
- Have you ever gone through a confusing time in life and not realized what God was doing until years later? How did you respond in the moment? What did you learn after it was over?
- How does Jesus make life make sense?

18.

Just Say Thank You

Bible Reading: Romans 15:13

Some people can't take a compliment.

For example, a friend walks up to you. You say, "Hey, love your jacket!"

"This old thing? No, it's ugly. It's old. I bought it at a garage sale. I'm going to go home and line my bird cage with it."

And inside you're thinking, *Well, I used to like it. But since you talked it down so much, now I'm not sure—*

Or you say to a coworker, "Good job on that speech, dude! That was perfect. So great." But he takes it all wrong, and says, "I know you could have done better. Sorry. It should have been you up there. I'm sorry."

And you're like, *Really? You could have just said, "Thank you."* Then you make a mental note not to ever pay that guy a compliment again because he's too insecure to take it.

Or here's another one. This one is specific to us spiritual, Jesus-following people. You tell someone, "You are an amazing woman. You are generous, you are gifted, you are—"

"No!" She interrupts you, almost shouting. "It's not about me. It's about him." She points upward, piously. "I don't deserve the glory. It's all God."

That sounds so spiritual. But it's not.

It's weird.

Why is it often so hard for us to take a compliment? I think it's because we don't want to seem proud or arrogant. We know we are weak and that the reason for our successes is the grace of God. So we deflect praise. We reject credit. We refuse compliments.

It's true that God ultimately deserves the glory for all good things. After all, he created us. He gave us the talents and abilities and opportunities that led to our successes. But God isn't insecure. He's happy to share the credit with you. He's not going to fry you with lightning or turn you into a pillar of salt because you said thank you to a compliment.

Actually, this kind of self-deprecating "humility" is often nothing but pride in disguise. It's false humility.

Why? Because at its core, pride is simply thinking too much about ourselves. It's focusing too much on who we are, what we need, and what we can do. When we constantly tell everyone how terrible we are, we are still operating out of pride because we are still making it all about us. It might sound more humble, but it's not. Insecurity is simply the flip-side of pride.

Sometimes taking a compliment graciously can be the greatest demonstration of humility. It shows that we are secure and confident in who God made us to be. I think God would like to pay us compliments regularly. He would love to boost our self-esteem, to encourage us, and to make us believe we are awesome and full of potential.

But that's tough, because many of us are really, really committed to our weird concept of humility. So we insist we aren't worthy to do the great things God calls us to do—which is true, by the way, but completely irrelevant. God makes us sufficient, not our abilities.

Or we play up our weaknesses and refuse to acknowl-edge our strengths—which is ungrateful and actually insulting to God, because he made us and he's proud of his handiwork. Or we get stingy with our compliments, lest we become accomplices in giving someone else an inflated ego—which is just dumb, because their level of humility is their business before God, not ours.

Groveling, insulting ourselves, or refusing responsi-bility doesn't point people to God. It points them to us. It highlights our insecurity and self-centeredness.

God wants you to enjoy who you are and what you were created to do. The pride you feel from a job well done is the same type of pride God felt when he made the universe.

"Then God looked over all he had made, and he saw that it was very good!" (Genesis 1:31). If pride is a sin—which it is—God can't be prideful. Yet here we find him patting himself on the back for a job well done.

As we trust in God, we gain confidence in ourselves. We become secure, stable, solid people because we know how trustworthy God is. That kind of confidence is the opposite of arrogance. It's authentic humility. It's recognizing who we are *in Jesus*. Paul wrote this in his letter to the Roman church:

> I pray that God, the source of hope, will fill you completely with joy and peace because you trust in him. Then you will overflow with confident hope through the power of the Holy Spirit. (Romans 15:13)

Paul wasn't saying that we should put our trust in ourselves or take all the credit for ourselves. He was saying that our confidence comes from God. God is the source of hope, joy, and peace. If the Holy Spirit—the presence and power of God—is in our lives, we will naturally be confident, positive, courageous people.

So how about you? Can you take a compliment?

The answer says a lot about how much you trust in God.

Questions for Reflection:

- Would you consider yourself a confident person? Why or why not?
- How does trusting God increase your self-confidence?
- What are some specific things God would like to compliment you on?

19

Boogey Boy

Bible Reading: Psalm 61:1-4

The first time I went boogey boarding was also the last. I was eleven years old, and my parents were speaking in a camp in Honolulu. My dad was busy preparing for his message, so he sent his sweet, helpless son to catch some waves on the beach.

In the Northwest we have a lot of water. We just don't go in it because it's freezing. So nothing had prepared me for the force of nature that is the Hawaiian surf. In retrospect, there was no way this could have ended well.

The locals were friendly. "Watch out for the coral reef, bro," they told me. I had no idea what a reef was. But I was about to find out. So I was out there, rolling up and down over swells, watching these guys do their thing. Finally I decided to try it. A wave was coming, so I pointed my board at the shore and caught the wave. The rush, the thrill, the power—it was awesome.

Until it broke on top of me.

The wave was maybe three to four feet tall, but it might as well have been thirty-four feet tall. It destroyed me. My board apparently ceased to exist. I found myself doing what I affectionately call the death roll, tumbling and bouncing through the foam and surf.

Then I discovered the coral reef, up close and personal. The wave dragged me across it, chafing and cutting my chest and hands. Finally my brain kicked into gear. I realized I had to get out of the wave. *Now.* So I tried to stand up. But I couldn't. The wave was controlling me. It was holding me down.

That's when panic really hit.

Eventually the wave relented, and I came shooting out of the water, screaming and yelling. "Help me! I'm going to die!" I've always had a flair for the dramatic.

Then I looked down and realized I was standing in about eighteen inches of water. I glanced up at all the locals, floating on their boards. They were laughing at me hysterically. As I made my way toward the shore, I can't describe the relief it was to feel solid ground beneath my feet. I've been a pool kind of guy ever since.

Like the Hawaiian surf, sometimes life has a way of overwhelming us. Circumstances beyond our control can knock us over, hold us under, and threaten to drown us. Sometimes it feels like we haven't yet recovered from one wave when along comes another. In moments like that, we try desperately to regain our footing. We search for solid ground. We know that if we can just get our feet firmly planted, we'll be okay.

David understood that desperate, panicked feeling, maybe even better than we do. Time after time he found himself in impossible scenarios and overwhelming circumstances. Maybe that's why he wrote this:

> *From the end of the earth I will cry to You,*
> *When my heart is overwhelmed;*
> *Lead me to the rock that is higher than I.*
>
> *For You have been a shelter for me,*
> *A strong tower from the enemy.*
> *I will abide in Your tabernacle forever;*
> *I will trust in the shelter of Your wings.*
>
> (Psalm 61:2–4 NKJV)

David uses a lot of metaphors here. High rock. Shelter. Strong tower. Tabernacle. Wings. He doesn't mention boogey boards and coral reefs, but had he ever been to Hawaii, I'm sure he would have.

David knew that the solid ground he longed for was found in God alone. God was his rock. God was his shelter and his protection. In the middle of the swirling, churning, currents of life, God was immovable. God was solid.

Often we think that peace and tranquility will come when our troubles disappear. We want the waves to go away and the current to vanish. If our circumstances would just change, we believe, we would find solid ground. We would regain our footing and stability.

Sometimes that happens—and when it does, it's wonderful. But often, our situation doesn't improve. At least not right away. For what seems an impossibly long time, our heads are held underwater, our souls are banged and bruised, and we struggle to catch every breath of air. But here's the deal. Our physical, literal situation doesn't have to change in order for us to find rest and safety. We have a spiritual rock who is with us wherever we go.

Like David, we have instant and permanent access to the one person in the entire universe who can never be moved. When everything around is shifting and uncertain, God is our solid ground. God helps us find our footing in the foam and froth and surf of life. And unlike the peanut gallery on that Hawaiian beach, God doesn't mock our missteps. He doesn't despise us when we mess up or wipe out. He doesn't get frustrated with our failures.

It's just the opposite. He is drawn to our desperation and attracted by our anxiety. God is a God of the overwhelmed. Of the trapped. Of the helpless and hopeless. That's why throughout the Bible we find references to God watching out for orphans and widows. In the Hebrew culture, they were defenseless. They had no one to rescue them, so God himself promised to intervene.

Maybe you are in an impossible, overwhelming situation. You can't find your footing, and you are thinking, *If God doesn't help me, I'm toast. I'm finished. Game over.*

God hears your cry. He knows your need. It may not happen when or how you expect it, but God will be your refuge and your rock. He will be your solid ground.

Life doesn't always make sense. I can't explain why we get our feet swept out from under us sometimes, or why circumstances don't always line up with what we expect God to do.

But I've learned this: God knows how to rescue those he loves.

Questions for Reflection

- In general, is it hard for you to depend on God for help? Why or why not? Does God expect you to face life alone?
- What do you think is going through God's mind when you are in impossible, overwhelming situations?
- In what practical ways can you make God your rock and your shelter when tough times come?

20

Breaking News

Bible Reading: Psalm 46:1–11

If you ever want to enjoy a little emotional whiplash, just check the news. Guaranteed, you'll experience every sentiment and feeling known to humanity in a matter of seconds. You go from watching a clip about your football team heading to the Super Bowl to images of war-ravaged refugees on the other side of the world. Stories of heroism, greed, tragedy, humor, generosity, and evil are juxtaposed in a mind-numbing stream.

Talk about emotionally confusing. Plus, the stories are interrupted by commercials that target what can only be called first-world problems. One second you are looking at heart-wrenching images of an earthquake somewhere, and the next you are trying to figure out why a lizard is selling car insurance.

It seems that bad news is more readily available now than ever before in the history of humanity. You don't even have to look for it. Technology delivers it to you wherever you are at. You can be perusing the sales rack at Nordstrom's and get a breaking news alert on your phone about a missing airliner with hundreds of human lives on board. Then mere minutes later you get updates on Oscar nominees and about who is wearing whom on the red carpet.

It's jarring. It's bizarre.

I'm not criticizing advertisers or newscasters. I'm not ranting about the times we live in or the media outlets that feed our appetite for information. This is simply the nature of culture and technology. But if we aren't careful, it can get unhealthy. It can get overwhelming. Between the barrage of bad news and the interrupting talking lizards, it starts to feel like too much. I can't comprehend it all or carry it all. It breaks my heart and messes with my emotions.

Shutting down and shutting out is not the solution either. We all know that. God made us to be compassionate and loving. We are supposed to care. Something within us wants to help, to give, to change the scenarios we see.

An anonymous quote that is sometimes attributed to Mother Teresa goes like this: "May God break my heart so completely that the whole world falls in." That is a beautiful yet haunting thought. How can we care that much? How can we carry that much?

Somehow, we have to care without being crushed. We

have to hurt *for* humanity without giving up hope *in* humanity. Our hearts need to break in compassion but not in despair.

There is only one sufficient and sustainable answer: trust in God. The book of Psalms says this:

> *God is our refuge and strength,*
> *always ready to help in times of trouble.*
> *So we will not fear when earthquakes come*
> *and the mountains crumble into the sea.*
> *Let the oceans roar and foam.*
> *Let the mountains tremble as the waters surge!*
> (Psalm 46:1–3)

Life is going to involve some bad news at times. But God is in control. He is our source of hope and strength. I don't think God designed us to have instant access to every evil and woe in the world. He didn't build us to carry the weight of the world on our shoulders. It will crush us every time.

That's *his* job.

Jesus is the hope of humanity. Jesus is the Savior of the world. We are not. It's really helpful if we keep that straight. That doesn't mean we tune out the woes the world is facing. We don't make light of the sin and suffering that surrounds us. We don't ignore other people in the name of focusing on God.

Actually it's just the opposite.

I've found that the more I trust God, the larger my heart

for other people grows. He increases my capacity to love, to give, and to believe. Understanding his power and goodness expands my sphere and my personal capacity to engage with a hurting world.

I can't solve the woes of the world. I can't even fully grasp them or emotionally process them. But God can. And to the extent that I trust in him, I can love the world and participate in its healing. God is the most powerful, sustainable source of hope that exists.

God loves the world far more than we do. He loves humanity so much that he sent his Son to die for us. God already provided the answer for sin and pain and death. And it's not a program or a political party or a code of conduct—it's a person.

It's Jesus.

Tragedies and atrocities, disasters and disease and destruction—they should break our hearts with compassion. But they should also remind us that we have a hope that is bigger than bad news. We have a God who is actively at work to seek and save those who are lost, to turn the tide of evil, and to restore the world to a relationship with him.

Jesus is our hope.

Questions for Reflection

- Have you ever felt overwhelmed by problems in the world that seemed too big to bear? Why did you feel that way? How did you respond?
- How does trusting God help us be more proactive and engaged with the problems around us?
- How is Jesus the hope for humanity?

SECTION 3

LIFE IS TO BE AT PEACE WITH GOD AND YOURSELF

21.

The Principal's Office

Bible Reading: Hebrews 4:16

As a kid, were you ever called into the principal's office with no explanation of what the meeting was about? Or as an adult, were you ever called into your boss's office mysteriously? You had no warning. No signs of an impending storm. All you knew was that you'd been summoned, and it wasn't optional. You had been requested to appear before someone who could inflict dire consequences upon you if they so chose.

Instantly your mind replayed every chance encounter, every flippant word, every possible misunderstanding. *What did I do?* you wondered. *Why am I here? This is not going to end well . . .*

You had no idea why you were being subpoenaed, so you automatically assumed it was something bad. You were going to be reprimanded or fired or expelled. Or at least chewed out. So you formulated potential defenses for every possible infraction. Your mental playbook would have put an NFL defensive coordinator to shame.

You sat down in front of the desk. You were sweating. Secretly, of course, because you were trying to act innocent. Which was weird because as far as you knew you *were* innocent, so you shouldn't have to act that way—but apparently the person didn't think you were, so you wondered if you looked innocent enough, and that only made you look guiltier than ever. It was so confusing.

Even more confusing, the authority looked at you and *smiled*. Then—of all things—he or she paid you a compliment. And then dismissed you.

No correction, no rebuke, no beatings or blood or violence.

You were stunned. You hardly knew how to respond. "Um, wow. Thank you? I'll just be leaving now."

It seemed too good to be true. Inside you half-suspected it was a trap. So you hurried away before the person could think of something you'd done wrong and called you back.

Okay, maybe your story didn't have such a fairy-tale ending. Maybe you were guilty, and they dropped the hammer on you, and things got really nasty, and you spent the rest of your life in counseling. Just work with me here.

There is something about being in the presence of authority that makes us take ourselves and our performance seriously. And that's not a bad thing, at least when it's at a healthy level. It's respect. Honor. Responsibility. The Bible sometimes uses the words *fear* or *awe*. These are good attitudes to have toward God and toward others who have positions of responsibility over us.

The fact that we respect our authorities isn't a problem. But the fact that we so quickly jump to the conclusion they are mad at us is. Especially when we impose that conclusion on God.

I'm not here to defend or critique the authorities in your life. Between parents, teachers, and bosses, most of us have had both negative and positive experiences. But it's worth asking yourself this: *In light of how I've been treated by authorities in the past, how do I feel about God right now? Do I always think I'm in trouble? Or can I approach him confidently?*

The writer to the Hebrews understood the human tendency to hide from God in fear and guilt. He wrote this:

So let us come boldly to the throne of our gracious God. There we will receive his mercy, and we will find grace to help us when we need it most. (Hebrews 4:16)

Here's the complicated part. When it comes to God, we really *are* guilty. We've made mistakes, and we deserve to be called out and punished. We know it and God knows it. So we approach God, nervous and defensive, bracing ourselves for the worst. But he smiles at us. And tells us he loves us. And that he thinks we are wonderful.

It seems too good to be true.

The Bible is very clear: because of Jesus' death and resurrection, we have been forgiven. Past, present, and future sins are dealt with. We don't need to wonder and worry about when we are going to be called on the carpet for our failures.

That doesn't mean God ignores our sins or their consequences, of course. If we are unaware of what we are doing wrong, or if we insist on continuing in error even when we know better, God is faithful to step in and help us break the cycle of sin and failure. But his overall attitude toward us is one of peace, acceptance, and approval. We don't need to be afraid of him. We don't need to hide from him. We need to go to him for help.

When you approach God—maybe in church, or in prayer, or while reading your Bible—how do you imagine the encounter will go down? Do you expect the worst? Do you assume he's ticked off at you? Do you think he's preparing to blast you with a catalog of all your sins and mistakes and flaws?

Do you play defense, giving him all the reasons why you aren't as guilty as you feel? Or do you approach him in boldness, in grace, and in mercy, expecting to receive the help you need?

God is not against you and he's not out to trap you, humiliate you, expel you, or fire you.

He is smiling at you. He's applauding you. And he's telling you how proud he is of your efforts.

Let down your guard, and come boldly into his "office" today.

You'll be glad you did.

Questions for Reflection

- How have your experiences with authorities in your life affected your relationship with God? Is there anything about your view of God that needs to change?
- When you feel guilty for something you've done, do you tend to approach God or avoid God? Why? Is that the correct response?
- What are three things—or more—that God is proud of you for?

22.

Dirt Ninja

Bible Reading: Philippians 3:3-11

When I was nineteen, I became a custodian at my church. Some people might call us janitors, but I prefer to think of myself as a "sanitary professional." Or maybe "dirt ninja." That has a nice ring to it.

Oddly, the day I applied for the job, the person interviewing me didn't seem to care too much about my résumé. No one asked what my GPA had been in high school. No one was interested in whether I had a doctorate or a master's degree or a bachelor's degree—or probably even a high school diploma, for that matter. They didn't need to know how many years of experience I had or what professional achievements I could list.

The lack of interest in my résumé wasn't because my parents were the pastors, by the way. Nepotism was not in their vocabulary when I was growing up. If anything, my family connections worked against me because I was a readily available source of free labor. God is healing my heart, though. I'm not that bitter.

The reason my résumé was irrelevant was because you don't need an education or experience to scrub toilets. Since I was older than sixteen and not currently in a coma, I qualified.

No résumé required.

Have you ever met people who give you their verbal résumés within moments of starting up a conversation? It doesn't matter what you were originally talking about. Somehow they manage to mention where they went to college, what books they have written, which celebrities they hang out with, where they go on vacation, and how big their houses are.

I say "people," but I've done it too. Often we do it because inside we feel insecure and unqualified. It's less about impressing others and more about convincing *ourselves* of our worth. And I think most people see through that.

The crazy thing is that sometimes we approach God the same way. Some of us think that every time we pray, we have to give God our résumés. We have to impress him into blessing us by listing how hard we've worked and how spiritually awesome we are. But that's illogical. We can't impress God with our performance. Whatever we can do, Jesus can do better. And he already has.

That's exactly why we don't have to worry about earning

God's favor or deserving his love. Jesus already did that. Jesus lived the life we could never live: free from faults or mistakes or sins. We don't have to prove our worth to him. We don't have to justify our petitions or earn his favor.

The apostle Paul understood this principle. Before he met Jesus, he was far more spiritually "qualified" than most people. He was a Pharisee. He came from a perfect family. He was zealous for God. He adhered to strict laws of holiness and carefully avoided even the appearance of sin. Yet inside, he was far from God. Here's what Paul had to say about his former résumé:

> I once thought these things were valuable, but now I consider them worthless because of what Christ has done. Yes, everything else is worthless when compared with the infinite value of knowing Christ Jesus my Lord. For his sake I have discarded everything else, counting it all as garbage, so that I could gain Christ and become one with him. I no longer count on my own righteousness through obeying the law; rather, I become righteous through faith in Christ. (Philippians 3:7–9)

When we put our trust in Jesus, his résumé becomes ours. His achievements and accomplishments and victory become ours. We can approach God with confidence not because of what we've done or even who we are but because of what Jesus has done and who he is.

It's relatively easy to believe that when we first start following Jesus. At the time, we knew we were sinners. We knew we needed grace. But time passes. As we follow Jesus, we start to see changes. We find freedom from a lot of the external sins, addictions, and habits that used to hold us back. We become better people. Holier people. More spiritual people. We accomplish things that we know God is proud of, things that are genuinely amazing.

That's a good thing, of course. Our character and our actions should reflect the fact that Jesus is in our lives. But as our spiritual résumés get more impressive, sometimes we start to depend on them too much. Sometimes we forget that we were saved and called by grace, and that grace will always be the way we draw near to God.

Sometimes these newfound résumés produce pride because we get impressed with ourselves and assume God should be too. Sometimes we think our qualifications are so incredible that we deserve all the blessings God gives us and more. We become spiritual Pharisees, like Paul was.

Other times, we end up drowning in insecurity. Deep inside, we suspect we are letting God down. We are afraid we don't qualify, we don't measure up, we don't deserve our position.

Ironically, this sense of failure can grow stronger the longer we walk with God—if we don't keep our eyes on Jesus. Why? Because the more we grow spiritually, the more we notice how much we still need to grow. We become more aware of how much we still lack and of how hard it is to change. As a result, although we are probably holier, more loving, and more selfless than ever, we might still feel like failures.

The answer isn't to try harder or be better. The answer isn't to convince God or ourselves or anyone else that we have the best résumés around. The answer is to put our faith in Jesus.

When it comes to being accepted by God, Jesus is all the qualification we need.

Questions for Reflection

- Do you ever feel like a spiritual failure? How do you deal with those thoughts?
- Is it hard for you to believe God accepts you unconditionally? Why or why not?
- How does the fact that Jesus is your qualification make it easier for you to handle your weaknesses and failures? Does his acceptance motivate you to improve? Why or why not?

23.

Dodging the Question

Bible Reading: Psalms 42–43

There is a particular skill I possess that often comes in handy. I'm not necessarily proud of it, but it's definitely useful. Over the years, I've practiced and honed it more than I'd like to admit.

It's the fine art referred to as "dodging the question." I have a God-given, instinctive ability to avoid issues that I don't want to deal with by talking my way around them. I've always been a talker. So I'm sure this started in my childhood with my long-suffering parents. Throughout my childhood, my teen years, and right up into my marriage, I have successfully ducked and dodged and redirected innumerable questions that hit too close to home.

Things like, "Do you know who broke that window?" "Why is there broccoli in the toilet?" "How did your basketball uniform end up in the microwave?" "Have you seen the neighbor's cat?"

I discovered long ago that if I talk long enough and loud enough, the interrogator will usually forget the original question. Or lose interest and walk away. Either way, it's a win for me. My reasoning and arguments might be invalid and empty of substance, but I, for one, am always fully convinced that they are both true and weighty. What I lack in logic, I make up for in volume, conviction, and oratory. You can be praying for Chelsea, if you think of it.

It's one thing to engage in verbal trickery to get out of dealing with awkward questions. But sometimes we do something similar with the hard questions of life. We all have them: inner doubts and demons and fears. Thoughts that steal our peace and joy.

Why do I feel guilty? Am I a failure? Why am I lonely? What am I so afraid of? Am I important? Does anyone care about me? Will I ever be successful? Will I ever find love?

Those are difficult questions. Painful questions. They touch on issues of identity, trauma, and fear that are often easier to just ignore. So we try to distract ourselves with friends or work or fun. We medicate ourselves. We drink too much coffee. We do whatever it takes to dodge the questions that rattle around in our heads. But we can't evade them forever. We can't bluff them into submission. When we are alone with our thoughts, the questions are still there.

How do we respond? If dodging the questions doesn't work, how do we answer them?

We have to face them.

It's that simple. God wants us to deal with the things that are stealing our peace and disturbing our rest. Here's the key: we don't have to face them alone. We don't have to sort through the insecurities and failures from our past by ourselves. We don't have to confront the fears of the future in our own strength.

God is our source of peace, and he will help us find peace. He isn't afraid of the tough questions. He isn't embarrassed by our vulnerability or offended by our anger. He invites us to turn to him, to find strength in him.

The best part about turning to God in the face of life's tough questions is this: a lot of our questions end up answering themselves. It's hard to explain, but it's true. The closer we get to God and the more we comprehend his love, goodness, and acceptance, the less we struggle with our own doubts and insecurities.

I think the reason this happens is because, ultimately, the answer we are looking for isn't inside ourselves. The answer is a person, and his name is Jesus. Lasting and authentic peace doesn't come from knowing all the answers to all the questions. It comes from knowing the Answer.

That might sound simplistic, but it's true. Jesus makes life make sense. He is the one who knows us best. The one who knows the answers to our darkest questions. The one who created us, who designed us, who watches over us, and who walks us through the questions of life.

Professional counseling has its place, as does personal soul-searching and asking advice from friends or spiritual leaders. But helpful as those things are, they aren't enough if we don't first know God as our peace.

David understood human emotion. He knew what it was like to wrestle with doubts and fears. But he also knew how to turn his mind toward God. He knew that even when his emotions and thoughts betrayed him, God was his source of peace.

Why am I discouraged?
Why is my heart so sad?
I will put my hope in God!
I will praise him again—
my Savior and my God!

Now I am deeply discouraged,
but I will remember you . . .
(Psalm 42:5–6)

If you are struggling with unanswered questions, don't avoid them. But don't stress out over answering them, either. Turn to God. Find peace in him.

Then walk out the process of discovery with him by your side.

Let God forever be your source of perfect peace.

Questions for Reflection

- What are some difficult questions you have struggled with? For example, questions about your worth, your identity, your relationships, your past, or your future?
- Is it possible to have peace even if all your questions aren't answered perfectly? Why or why not?
- How does knowing God and focusing your thoughts on him help you deal with the confusion and complexity of life?

24.

Why Are You Not Freaking Out?

Bible Reading: Psalm 127:1-2

One of the occupational hazards of being a pastor is that you can't skip church to watch football. Okay, I did go to the Super Bowl once—when the Seahawks were playing. But that was the exception.

In the interest of full disclosure, however, I should admit there is a room off the church stage where I go between services to prep for the next service. But if there's a big game on, there is a significant probability I am not studying or praying. I'm squeezing in a few minutes of game time.

If I really want to watch a game from start to finish, though, I have to watch the replay that night or the next day. And I've noticed something. There is much less tension surrounding the game when you already know who wins. That has its benefits. It's better for your blood pressure, for example. And your screams don't scar your children for life.

But without a doubt I prefer to watch games live. I love the uncertainty, the drama, the adrenaline, and the angst. So when I do get a chance to watch a game in real time, especially when it's an important game, you'd better believe that I am verbally and physically engaged. I am the 12th man, whether I'm at home or at the stadium or pretending to study between church services.

Here's what gets me every time, though. Invariably there are people around who are consistently calm, composed, and uncommunicative. Even when our team is losing and the game is on the line. Even when we score an impossible touchdown after a trick play never attempted before in the history of football.

I don't understand it. How can these people just sit there? How can they stay silent when our team needs our chants, our yells, our physical demonstrations of loyalty and passion? For some, it's their personality. But let's be honest. Most of the time, it's because they don't care that much. If they did, they'd be yelling and crying and high-fiving and throwing things right beside me.

That's the nature of sports. But when it comes to life, I've discovered that screaming and kicking don't really help. Stressing out and freaking out are not that productive. Technically they don't help in football either, but let's not go there right now.

Life has a way of producing far more drama than a sports game. And people expect us to react emotionally and verbally. When life appears to be falling apart around us, people assume our demeanors and attitudes should reflect that. If they don't, people conclude the same thing I do when I see silent sports fans: that we don't care. That we are passive. That we are disengaged and disinterested. That we don't grasp the reality and gravity of our situations.

In the midst of the uncertainties of life, it seems that stress, worry, and fear aren't just inevitable reactions. They seem to be *responsible* reactions. After all, we need to foresee danger. We need to plan for adversity. We need to be ready for anything. We need to be wise. The Bible has a lot to say about all those things. But it also has a lot to say about living in God's peace. About resting in him, trusting him, and having faith in him.

How do we behave responsibly without going off the deep end emotionally? Or let me say it this way: How do we reconcile wisdom and peace?

The answer? We don't.

Wisdom and peace aren't opposing principles that have to constantly be held in balance. They aren't enemies. They are both found in *Jesus*. Jesus is wisdom, and Jesus is peace. In him, we can live both responsibly and restfully.

Solomon, known in the Bible as the wisest man to have ever lived, figured this out. Despite his wisdom, wealth, intelligence, and power, he knew that ultimately God was in control. More than his abilities or possessions, it was this knowledge that gave him peace. Here is what he wrote about it:

> *Unless the Lord builds a house,*
>   *the work of the builders is wasted.*
> *Unless the Lord protects a city,*
>   *guarding it with sentries will do no good.*
> *It is useless for you to work so hard*
>   *from early morning until late at night,*
> *anxiously working for food to eat;*
>   *for God gives rest to his loved ones.*
>
> (Psalm 127:1–2)

That almost sounds irresponsible—but it's not. It's a life lived from a place of peace, from a certainty that God is on our side and things will work out.

When you are at peace, not everyone will understand you. Some people will even criticize you. "Don't you realize the world is falling apart? Don't you understand the economy is tanking? Don't you care that life as we know it is going to change?" They'll think you are clueless, indifferent, even lazy.

In reality, true peace will make you wiser and more responsible than ever. You'll have a clearer perspective of what to do and how to do it. You'll understand what part

God plays and what part you play. You'll have the mental and emotional energy to not only face challenges but to triumph in them and enjoy life along the way.

Peace is not the same thing as passivity. And rest is not the same thing as irresponsibility. Peace and wisdom find their nexus, their connecting point, in Jesus.

Maybe you are facing challenges right now, and you're wondering how to respond. I'm not here to tell you what peace and wisdom will look like in your case. Every person and every situation is unique. But I can point you to Jesus. And as you seek him and listen to him and respond to him, you'll figure out how to face life's challenges with resourcefulness, strength, passion, and diligence—and from a place of authentic peace and rest.

Our individual reactions to the agony and ecstasy of sports are a personality thing. So I'll keep right on shouting and jumping on furniture, if you don't mind. But when it comes to life, let's let God build our future. Let's let God watch over our present.

Let's find our rest and peace in him, no matter what the world around us looks like.

Questions for Reflection

- What challenges or worries are you facing right now? Do you think you are handling them properly?
- What does the phrase "God gives rest" in Psalm 127 mean to you? What does God's rest look like?
- Do you need more wisdom, more peace, or both? How can you let Jesus be the source for what you need?

25.

The Road Not Taken

Bible Reading: Philippians 4:6-7

Do you have a dream job? By "dream job" I'm not talking about something you seriously intend to do, though. I'm thinking more of a fantasy occupation. Something you would only consider in an alternate universe where you didn't have bills to pay or kids to feed or retirement to plan for. It's something totally different from what you actually do, but you know if you did it, you'd love it and you'd be really good at it.

I do. I could totally see myself as a personal shopper. In case you don't know what that is, it's a person who puts together outfits for people who don't like to shop or maybe don't have time to shop—using *their* credit cards.

Really? That's a *job*? How awesome would that be? I love shopping, both for myself and for others. I get pumped helping my family and friends find outfits they love and that look amazing on them. I would be perfect at that job.

I have no immediate plans to give up pastoring and speaking, in case you were wondering. I love what I do. But sometimes I still wonder, *What if? What if I had gone into fashion? What would it be like to have taken a different path in life? To have made different choices?*

If we are honest with ourselves, we live a lot of our lives under the seductive sway of *what if.* I don't mean that we are bitter, angry, regretful people—I don't regret becoming a pastor at all. Becoming a personal shopper isn't my backup plan in case this whole pastoring thing doesn't work out. I just mean that sometimes we spend a lot of time second-guessing ourselves. Wondering about what it would be like if we had made different choices. Wishing we could go back in time and try it again.

There is a place for evaluating the past, of course. If we make mistakes, we should learn from them. That's wisdom. Our mistakes are some of our best teachers. And yes, the future is to some extent under our control. I'm not advocating that we forget where we came from or lose focus on where we are going. Please don't misunderstand me here.

But we can only *live in* today. The past is gone and the future is not guaranteed. We have to make the most of each moment, and we can't do that if we are constantly looking back and wondering if we should have taken a different path. The poet Robert Frost wrote this in his poem "The Road Not Taken."

> *I shall be telling this with a sigh*
> *Somewhere ages and ages hence:*
> *Two roads diverged in a wood, and I—*
> *I took the one less traveled by,*
> *And that has made all the difference.[1]*

The poem is a commentary on the power of choice. Our decisions might seem small in the moment, but they direct our lives. Someday we'll look back on them and see the difference they made. But right now, we can't see everything that lies down the road. And that fact can either stress us out or make us lean completely on God. It's our choice.

Paul referenced the past-present-future components of life in this well-known passage on peace:

Don't worry about anything; instead, pray about everything. Tell God what you need, and thank him for all he has done. Then you will experience God's peace, which exceeds anything we can understand. His peace will guard your hearts and minds as you live in Christ Jesus. (Philippians 4:6–7)

---

1   "The Road Not Taken" is in the public domain.

He said "tell God what you need" (future) and "thank him for all he has done" (past). The result will be an ongoing experience of God's peace in the present.

Sometimes I think we are too quick to assign labels to our choices. We make a decision, then something unexpected happens and all of sudden we think that we blew it. We label it a bad decision and kick ourselves for being so dumb. But often, we simply don't know. Even when we think we do. We might not know if a particular choice was a mistake or a win for years. Maybe not ever.

A better approach would be to look at the past and thank God for it. Even the tough parts. Even the mistakes and the pain. Not out of some masochistic idea that God wants us to suffer, but out of a recognition that God is so big and so good and so completely sovereign that he takes even our blunders and uses them for our good. One of the keys to living in peace is being able to rest in the fact that even in our free-will choices, God still takes care of us.

I know there are consequences for our actions. We shouldn't flippantly sin or purposefully make poor choices. I think we all agree on that. But if we think that every tiny choice is going to have eternal, unalterable, and possibly fatal consequences in our lives and the lives of those around us, the word *paranoid* won't even begin to describe us. We will live under the constant shadow of *what if,* and it will steal our hope and our faith for the paths we've chosen.

Spending too much time second-guessing the past can

keep us from changing things that need to be changed right now. Our insecurity about our decisions makes us hold on to things that are no longer working, because we think changing them would be admitting to failure.

But again—who's to say it was a failure? Maybe it was perfect for the moment, but it's time to move on. And if your new decision or path doesn't work down the road, change it again. Or even go back to the first path.

Whatever you do, do it fully convinced that God is guiding your steps, even if you don't see him or sense him.

Your future is in his hands, so his peace can permeate your present.

Questions for Reflection

- Do you second-guess your decisions very often? Why or why not?
- How can you learn from your mistakes without constantly living in the past?
- How does being grateful for your past help you have peace in your present and faith for your future?

26

Peace and Pebbles

Bible Reading: Romans 5:1-5

One of the more irritating sensations in life is to have a rock in your shoe. I'm sure it's happened to you. Maybe you rush out of the door into a day full of activities, only to realize within seconds that there is a pebble rolling around in your sneaker. How it got there, you have no idea. It wasn't there yesterday. And your shoes have been in the closet all night, not in a gravel quarry. But somehow this irritant, this aggressive grain of grit, inserted itself into your shoe and your life.

You're too busy or too distracted—or too lazy—to deal with it. That would require a multistep process, after all. Stop, bend over, untie shoe, take out rock, put shoe back on, tie shoe. Who has time for that? So you spend the rest of the day limping around. Periodically you stop and tap your shoe sideways on the ground in hopes the rock will dislodge and slide into a less uncomfortable place in your shoe.

That tiny stone, practically invisible, might as well be a boulder. It begins to rule your life. It dominates your thoughts. You don't want to stand or walk because subconsciously you know it will be waiting for you. You find yourself getting irritable and grumpy. You question the meaning of life and the existence of God. You start to harbor bitter thoughts toward rocks and cliffs and anything remotely stone-like. You consider running away from the pain and angst of life and moving to a cabin in Montana.

Finally you can't take it anymore. You take twelve seconds out of your life to remove the rock. Then you slide your shoe back on and stand up. Inside, you brace yourself in case nothing has changed. But the rock is gone, and the feeling of relief is palpable. It's massive. It's like you got a new lease on life. You wonder, *Why didn't I stop to take that out hours ago?*

Good question.

When it comes to our walk with God, something similar can happen. Without realizing it, small issues can work their way between God and us. Unresolved issues start to steal our joy and ruin our peace. They keep us from enjoying our walk with God like we should.

Yes, we still love God. Yes, our relationship with him is the best part of life. We aren't going to give up on God anytime soon. But the underlying, unresolved issues need to be addressed.

These figurative rocks in our shoes can be many things.

For example, maybe we had an expectation in a particular area of need in our lives. We prayed, we believed—and nothing happened. We feel like God let us down. Every time we try to believe for the future, there are nagging doubts in our minds. *Maybe God isn't good. Maybe he isn't watching out for me. Maybe he doesn't care.*

Or it could be an area of sin in our lives, a temptation that keeps getting the best of us. We know it's wrong, and we want to change. We've tried and failed and tried and failed again. We live with a sense of guilt, and it spoils our relationship with God.

If that's you, I'm not trying to minimize your struggle or your pain. I'm not going to tell you that it's as easy to fix as taking off your shoe and shaking out the offending pebble. And it's certainly going to take longer than twelve seconds. But I do want to say that in any relationship, a certain amount of confusion, miscommunication, and even offense is normal.

Peace doesn't mean avoiding all pain and misunderstanding. Peace is a lifestyle. It's a relationship. It's a commitment. Peace isn't so much absence of conflict as it is quick, consistent conflict *resolution.*

Peace with God is about walking through the good times and the bad, knowing that no matter what happens or how confusing things are, he is committed to our well-being.

God doesn't get his feelings hurt when we don't understand his decisions. And he doesn't get frustrated with us when we can't seem to get the victory over a character defect or temptation. God is bigger than that. He's more committed to us than that.

Paul pointed out that peace with God doesn't mean lack of difficulties—but it does mean we can have faith in his love for us.

> Therefore, since we have been made right in God's sight by faith, we have peace with God because of what Jesus Christ our Lord has done for us . . . We can rejoice, too, when we run into problems and trials, for we know that they help us develop endurance. And endurance develops strength of character, and character strengthens our confident hope of salvation. And this hope will not lead to disappointment. For we know how dearly God loves us, because he has given us the Holy Spirit to fill our hearts with his love. (Romans 5:1–5)

If there is anything hindering our walk with God, it's probably easier to deal with than we realize. But the answer isn't to ignore the pebble and just hope it will go away. It's to go to God with transparency and trust and make our peace with him.

Maybe you need to take time to address some issues between yourself and God. Issues of disappointment, of guilt, of fear, of doubt. Don't wait any longer. Don't limp through life, trying to ignore the fact that things between you and God aren't as comfortable as they could be.

God offers you true peace with him.

You'll be amazed how quickly God can bring healing to your heart and how fulfilling life is when the rocks are removed.

Questions for Reflection

- Are there any "pebbles" that might be hindering your walk with God? How can you deal with issues that threaten to affect your relationship?
- How is peace more than just living without conflict? Can you have conflict and misunderstandings and still live a lifestyle of peace?
- How do you think God reacts when you go to him with your misunderstandings or complaints about life?

27.

Lights Out

Bible Reading: John 14:27

Automated public restrooms are one of the more unappreciated advances of civilization. Can we just stop and celebrate that fact?

As a lifelong germaphobe, I will do nearly anything to avoid public restrooms. But sometimes that's the only option. In those moments, I appreciate the fact that I can get through the incident without touching any of the restroom fixtures.

But there is one automated function whose benefit is dubious at best. I am referring to the restroom lights. Some places have sensors that automatically turn off the lights if they don't detect any motion for a certain amount of time. And that time is never quite long enough.

Maybe it's happened to you. Without getting awkwardly descriptive, you are engaged in the activity for which you entered the restroom in the first place. Enough said. And suddenly the light goes off and you find yourself in pitch-blackness. But your brain doesn't register what is happening at first. You think someone turned off the lights on purpose. Or maybe the electricity went out. Or maybe the apocalypse is happening, and you are stuck—of all places—in a bathroom. *What a way to go,* you think. *If the rapture is real, how is this going to work? It's going to be awkward.*

Then you realize the sensor just forgot you were there. But now what? You are alone. It would be weird to scream for help. And at this point, obviously, your range of motion is fairly limited. But eventually you wave your arms or legs or head enough, and the light turns back on. And you resolve to never use public restrooms again because it's just too traumatic.

You are probably wondering what my point is here. I'm glad you asked.

That feeling of darkness and confusion is not limited to automated light sensors with short attention spans. If we are honest, we have a lot of "lights out" moments in life. One second, everything seems normal. Life is good, God is good, and the future is bright. Then without warning, the lights go out.

Maybe there's a serious illness in your family. Or the bank decides to foreclose on your home. Or you lose your job. Suddenly nothing makes sense. You thought you had it all figured out, you thought the future was guaranteed, but now you aren't so sure. Deep inside you know that God is still in control, but for some reason he's leaving you in the dark.

What just happened? What went wrong? Did I mess up? Is someone out to get me? Is this the apocalypse?

Often, it's none of the above. Especially the apocalypse part. We didn't make a mistake, and no one—God included—is out to get us. It's just the nature of life. It's the uncertainty of human existence. To be honest, I wish it weren't that way. I wish we could guarantee that life would be easy and predictable and well lit. But it's not. And that's why God's peace is so essential.

It's easy to be peaceful when the world around us is at rest. When we can see what's ahead and we are in control. But when chaos and fear clamor for our attention, we need true peace the most. Peace has to work even in the face of problems or it really isn't peace at all. Jesus told his disciples:

> Peace I leave with you, My peace I give to you; not as the world gives do I give to you. Let not your heart be troubled, neither let it be afraid. (John 14:27 NKJV)

In other words, they expected God's peace to look like the normal human idea of peace: absence of conflict, freedom from threats, lack of problems. But Jesus wanted them to know that his peace isn't limited to our temporary circumstances or human limitations. That's why his peace is so much better than ours. The peace of God doesn't depend on being able to see the future. It isn't based on being in charge of what is happening around us. It depends on who

God is. It is the result of his nature and character and promises. God is dependable and powerful, and he is committed to being with us no matter what.

We can't predict life, but we can predict that God won't leave us or forsake us.

We can't guarantee the future, but we can guarantee that God will be there.

And that's the greatest source of peace we could ask for.

Questions for Reflection

- Have you ever experienced a time when suddenly things were out of your control or beyond your understanding? Describe the circumstances. What emotions did you experience?
- In general is it hard for you to feel at peace when you can't see the future or don't understand the present? Why or why not?
- How is God's idea of peace better than our idea of peace?

28

Wait for It

Bible Reading: Psalm 130

I recently discovered the glorious phenomenon known as emoji. I know I'm about two years behind everyone else and that the emoji train left the station long ago, but I'm climbing onboard anyway. Every time I text someone, I find myself perusing emoji panels to find one or two or maybe ten that illustrate my message. It's awesome.

Texting is my favorite form of communication, other than talking face-to-face. I'm not great with e-mails. I don't have a personal Facebook page. And I gave up staying on top of Twitter and Instagram and other social media outlets a long time ago. And I don't think I've written an actual letter in decades, if ever.

But texting works for me—or at least it works better than other forms of communication. It has a lot of benefits.

You can be brief. You can be spontaneous. You don't have to spell or punctuate that well. And of course, you can use emoji. Those are all things that fit my personality. It's an all-around win.

One of my favorite parts is that you can answer at your leisure. You can take time to think about what you are going to say. Of course, that backfires sometimes, because you can take so much time to think that you forget to write back. I do that a lot, actually. Maybe I'm older than I think.

I find myself apologizing to people, because at some point they texted me, asking for advice or prayer or counsel. They poured out their hearts. They bared their souls.

But I never texted back.

I meant to, of course. I started to reply. They saw those little blue dots appear on their screen—but then I got distracted and never finished. And the dots disappeared. And along with them, their hopes and dreams. When they see me in person, they tell me about how they sat there, phones in hand, waiting for replies that never came. *Just wait for it,* they told themselves. *He's a pastor. He wouldn't forget about me.*

But sooner or later, dejected and disillusioned, they pocketed their phones and gave up on technology and humanity and Christianity. And it's all my fault. That might be a slight exaggeration. But it does illustrate an important principle. Sometimes we wait for other people to answer the questions and fill the holes in our hearts. But often, it doesn't happen. The people we are counting on let us down.

We are all human. We all have our share of needs and struggles. We get to help each other out a lot—that's part of the beauty of being human. But ultimately we are not the answer for one another's problems.

For example, maybe a friend texts me asking me for marriage advice, but what he doesn't know is that at that moment I happen to be in the middle of a not-so-mature "discussion" with my own wife. I don't text back because I'm in no shape to tell him how to fix his problems. I'm still working on mine.

Or maybe someone calls to ask for counsel for a business decision. But I don't take the call because I've got the flu, and I'm so happy on pain medication that I have no business giving advice to anyone about anything.

I'm not trying to make excuses or justify anything. I'm just being real. I can't be anyone's savior, because I need my own savior.

We will never be able to meet everyone's expectations. We will never be able to give people all the affirmation, the affection, and the answers they need. We can never *be* enough or *do* enough to truly satisfy other people. And on the flipside, no one and nothing out there will be able to do that for us, either. Not our spouses. Not our kids. Not our friends. Not our achievements or prosperity or fame or possessions.

I'm not saying those things are unnecessary. They are gifts from God, and they bring a lot of happiness and joy. But ultimately, they can't fill the voids in our hearts. They can't bring us lasting satisfaction or security. That's why Jesus came to earth. He is the Savior we are all looking for. He brings us peace with God and peace with ourselves. He shows us how to live fulfilled, satisfied lives. The Bible says in the book of Psalms:

> *I wait for the LORD, my whole being waits,*
> *and in his word I put my hope.*
> *I wait for the LORD*
> *more than watchmen wait for the morning,*
> *more than watchmen wait for the morning.*
> (Psalm 130:5–6 NIV)

If we hang our hat on the hope that our best friend will be with us forever, or that our kids will make us happy, or that our job will provide security, we are setting ourselves up for disappointment. If we are waiting for people and circumstances to make us feel fulfilled and complete, we're going to be waiting a long time.

But if we wait on God, we won't be disappointed. He will never forget about us. He will never abandon us. He provides the inner peace and completeness that we all need.

Maybe you've found yourself struggling lately to find happiness in your circumstances. Maybe the things you thought would bring you peace have come and gone, and the void is still there. Your longing for peace is normal, healthy, and right. God put it within you. But it was meant to lead you to *him*. He is the God of peace, and knowing him is the path to being at peace with yourself.

And that's worth waiting for.

Questions for Reflection

- Have you ever had a friend who seemed to always want more of you no matter how much you gave? Was that healthy? Why or why not?
- Why are family, friends, or accomplishments never enough to bring us lasting peace and fulfillment?
- How does finding peace with God help us find peace with ourselves?

29.

What's Your Point?

Bible Reading: Matthew 5:17–20

Some people love to start stories—they just don't know how to finish them. So they keep going. And going. And going.

I'm sure you've met a few of these people. They are great, sincere individuals, but they happen to talk a lot. After one or two encounters with them, you learn to avoid conversation unless you have at least an hour to talk. To listen, actually—it's mostly a monologue.

For example, maybe you run into one of these hyperverbal friends. You only have five minutes to spare, and you make the mistake of commenting on how hot the weather has been. That, of course, reminds him of a time when the weather was even hotter. Several minutes into the description of precisely how sweaty and miserable everyone was, he gets distracted recounting how his air conditioner died and leaked coolant on the floor, and how his wife thought the cat licked it and rushed her to the vet. But midway through that substory he diverges into a description of the veterinarian himself, a rather greasy fellow he suspects had escaped from prison. Then some random detail about the vet's tattoo reminds him of a sports story that took place a decade earlier, which was the coldest winter on record, and coincidentally his central heating happened to be broken at the time, which reminds him of the repairman who came to fix it . . .

To him, all of this is riveting and pertinent and hilarious information. But you long ago stopped hearing his words. All you can do is stare at his mouth, which seems to be moving in hypnotic slow motion. You mindlessly nod your head when he pauses for affirmation, and you pray silently, *God, please make it stop.*

You love the guy. But you just wish he'd get to the point.

Sometimes I think we approach the Bible the same way. The stories are fascinating. The poetry is stunning. The laws about leprosy and sores are, frankly, gross. The prophecies are a little freaky. The teachings of Jesus are life changing. The letters by Peter and Paul are inspiring. But taken all together, it can be overwhelming. And sometimes we might wonder, *What's the point?*

In Jesus' day, many people had concluded that the point of Scripture and the Law was behavior. It was performance. It was holiness. That was the message of the religious teachers of the day. They told people that God was a holy, vengeful God. Humanity was weak and sinful. So the law was needed to basically protect people from themselves.

Then Jesus showed up. He had an entirely different approach toward God, life, and the Law. He focused first on God's love, not people's behavior. He preached grace and good news and acceptance instead of guilt and condemnation. He revealed a God who was far more inclusive than exclusive.

That caused more than a few arguments with the Jewish religious leaders. In one instance, they accused Jesus of undermining the laws of Scripture. He replied:

> Don't misunderstand why I have come. I did not come to abolish the law of Moses or the writings of the prophets. No, I came to accomplish their purpose . . . But I warn you—unless your righteousness is better than the righteousness of the teachers of religious law and the Pharisees, you will never enter the Kingdom of Heaven! (Matthew 5:17, 20)

Jesus was saying they had it all wrong. They were so focused on obeying the *letter* of the Law that they had missed the *purpose* of the Law completely. They might have had the appearance of righteousness, but that wasn't what God was after at all. They had missed the point. On another occasion, Jesus summed up the message of the Scriptures this way.

You search the Scriptures because you think they give you eternal life. But the Scriptures point to me! Yet you refuse to come to me to receive this life. (John 5:39–40)

In other words, the point of God's revelation to humanity wasn't performance or holiness or rule keeping. The laws and prophecies weren't an end in themselves. They pointed to someone. And that *someone* was Jesus. All Scripture points to the eternal life and the relationship of love that we have with God through Jesus.

But here's what I've noticed. Sometimes as Jesus followers, we still get confused about the point of it all. We forget that Jesus is the center of our belief system, and we start to think it is our behavior. We end up reducing Christianity to what we do or don't do. We define ourselves through our actions. We measure our acceptance by God by our performance. We judge and accept others based on their behavior.

Like the religious leaders of Jesus' day, we miss the point.

Let me say it this way: Jesus didn't die to change our behavior. He died to change our relationship with God. He came to earth, lived a perfect life, died on the cross, and rose again to return us to the acceptance and friendship with God that we lost through sin. That's the point of Scripture— our restored relationship with God through Jesus.

Don't reduce the love of God and the sacrifice of Jesus to a list of dos and don'ts. Don't make your relationship with God about how well you behaved today. Make it about Jesus.

Make it about the fact that through him you have peace with God and peace with yourself.

Celebrate the gift of eternal life that is yours by grace through faith in Jesus.

Questions for Reflection

- Why do you think people sometimes make Christianity more about rules and behavior than about relationship with God?
- How can you focus more on Jesus in your day-to-day life?
- How does knowing that Jesus—not behavior or performance—is the point of everything affect your walk with God?

30.

Stop Staring at That

Bible Reading: 2 Corinthians 12:8-10

I have a well-documented issue with stains. Especially stains on clothing. I can't handle them. It's weird, it's wrong, it's OCD—I know all that. But it's real, and I can't change it.

When our kids were smaller and we would go out to eat as a family, Chelsea would always take extra clothing for them. She knew that if—or rather, when—they spilled something, I would no longer be able to eat. The soiled, stained offender would either have to sit there in his or her underwear, or we'd all leave early. Either option was preferable to cohabitating with a stain.

If I'm out with friends and a guy spills ketchup or something on his jacket, I can no longer focus on the conversation. All I can do is stare at the stain. It's a horrifying but fatal attraction. And I'm sure it comes across as creepy. Stalker Judah.

Or if I get a stain on my favorite shirt, it instantly becomes my least favorite shirt. It doesn't matter how expensive the garment or how faint the stain, I will throw it away or give it away immediately. It is dead to me.

When it comes to stains, if I can see it at all, it is all I can see.

That's how a lot of us are with our weaknesses. We can't seem to see past them. We talk about them, we pray about them, we work on them, and we fixate on them. We are convinced that if we can just fix what's wrong with us, we'll finally be happy. We'll be at peace with God and ourselves.

Somehow we've convinced ourselves that God expects perfection. But that's not true. God knows we have weaknesses, and he is okay with that. He's already made provision for them. As a matter of fact, he takes delight in being strong precisely where we are weakest.

The apostle Paul told the Corinthian church about a particular weakness that he was struggling with and how God responded to his prayer for help. The Bible doesn't say what the weakness was, and I think that was intentional. God wants us to understand that he is our source of strength in any deficiency. Paul wrote:

> Three different times I begged the Lord to take it away. Each time he said, "My grace is all you need. My power works best in weakness." So now I am glad to boast about my weaknesses, so that the power of Christ can work

through me. That's why I take pleasure in my weaknesses, and in the insults, hardships, persecutions, and troubles that I suffer for Christ. For when I am weak, then I am strong. (2 Corinthians 12:8–10)

Paul asked for help, but God refused to take the weakness away. That's a crazy thought. But apparently God wasn't as bothered by the issue as Paul was. He preferred to be strong in and through Paul's shortcoming.

I'm convinced that God is less limited by our weaknesses than by our refusal to believe in his strength. That is, our deficiencies and problems don't stop God at all. But when we refuse to look past them, when we limit ourselves and define ourselves by what we can't do, we end up hindering God's work in our lives.

Maybe you've read in the Bible how God told Moses to go to Egypt and rescue his people. The account is found in Exodus 4. To make a long story short, Moses didn't think he was up to the task. Time after time God told Moses he could do it, but each time Moses told God he couldn't. God even did multiple miracles in front of Moses, but it wasn't enough. Moses always had a reason why he wasn't the right guy for the job. He couldn't see past his imperfections.

So he told God no.

Bad idea.

The Bible says God got angry at him. What's fascinating to me is that God didn't get upset at Moses' weaknesses.

He already knew Moses wasn't the best orator around and that he had messed up in the past. But he chose him anyway.

What frustrated God was Moses' refusal to believe. It was Moses' inability to look past himself and see the power that was available to him through God. At one point in their conversation, Moses asked God to tell him his name. Moses knew that the Israelites would want to know who had sent him as their leader.

So God told Moses his name. He said, "I AM WHO I AM" (Exodus 3:14). Odd name. But God was making a point. He is anything and everything he needs to be, anywhere, and at any time. He doesn't depend on anyone and he is superior to everyone. He is more than enough for any need.

God's answer to Moses' insecurity wasn't to build his self-esteem. It wasn't to convince Moses that he was big enough or man enough for the job—not on his own, anyway. God's answer to Moses' identity issue was *himself.* Moses didn't need to worry about his lack, because God was more than sufficient. He shouldn't have been dissuaded by his inabilities, because God was more than able.

The same holds true for you and me. Yes, we all have problems and imperfections. God is working on them, and over time many of them will disappear. But in the meantime, we can be at peace with who we are, because God is our *I AM.* He is our source of strength.

Look past your stains and spots and sins, and focus on

Jesus. Listen to Jesus. Let his opinion of you define you, not your own.

And remember, God's power works best in your weakness.

Questions for Reflection

- What are some weaknesses or problems in your own life that you want to see changed? Are those things truly obstacles for God?
- Have you ever had trouble believing God could use you? Why or why not?
- What does it mean to you that God is your *I* AM? How does his sufficiency and strength help you in your weaknesses?

SECTION 4

LIFE IS TO ENJOY GOD

31.

Uh. May. Zing.

Bible Reading: Psalm 36:7-9

The word *amazing* is one of the most overused words in the English language. There's no doubt about it. I've had family members and staff members show me surveys to that effect, and I know exactly what they are trying to tell me: that I need to broaden my vocabulary. Expand my vernacular. Maybe employ some new superlatives. I am the poster child for overusing the term. I use it extravagantly and indiscriminately. My propensity to work the word *amazing* into any context is, quite frankly, amazing.

This dessert is amazing. The sunset is amazing. My wife is amazing. You are amazing. Oprah is amazing. That punt return was amazing. This facial cleanser is amazing.

Sometimes I subconsciously realize I am wearing out

the term, so I mix it up a bit. No, I don't change the word. I just emphasize different syllables.

UH-mazing

a-MAAAY-zing

Uh. May. Zing.

I don't do it flippantly, of course. I really do think a lot of things are amazing. Desserts are amazing—and for that matter, carbs in general. My spouse and sunsets and the Seahawks are amazing. And even certain beauty products are amazing. I'll admit that. I'm secure in who I am.

I overgeneralize good things, and I lump them all into the *amazing* category. On the flipside, I also find it too easy to overgeneralize negative things. Basically, anything that isn't amazing is terrible. It's rotten and horrible and doesn't deserve to exist.

Okay, that's not entirely true. But I do tend toward drama and flair and maybe some exaggeration.

I don't think I'm alone in my approach to life. I might be a bit more emotional than some people—or at least more adjective-challenged—but it's human nature to look at things dramatically and vividly. I'm sure you do it too. We don't just observe life from some neutral, detached vantage point: we *live* it. We participate in it. We experience it. It's colorful, crazy, and sometimes confusing. And it's beautiful.

Lack of energy, lack of desire, lack of interest in life, ambivalence—those are symptoms of depression. They are signs that something is wrong. It is our nature to live life to the fullest, to wring every last drop of fun and happiness out of what we do.

The odd thing is, when we look at God, sometimes we strip him of emotion. Sometimes we view him as cold, calculating, and clinical. We imagine someone who is distant and detached. Maybe we see him as a mad scientist of sorts, with a giant lab coat and oversized splash goggles, peering down from heaven to see how his experiments on the human race are playing out.

If we do imagine him in some emotional state, it's often a negative one. We think he is angry. Disappointed. Frustrated. Sad. But happy? Excited about life? Goofing off? Looking for fun? Playing? Laughing? Not so much. For many people, the mere thought of God giggling or cracking jokes seems wrong. Even blasphemous. Why would God goof off? He has so much to think about and worry about. Yet it's far closer to the biblical picture of God than some sour-faced, celestial party pooper.

We need to realize that our *joie de vivre*, our enjoyment of life, is not a human invention. We didn't create our love of living or our desire to find fulfillment and satisfaction in our existence.

God did.

Why? *Because he loves life too.*

And he made us in his image. It's no surprise that we enjoy life. That we desire fun and pleasure. That we love adrenaline and good food and late-night hangouts with friends. It's our nature, because it's God's nature. And through him, we are able to enjoy life to the fullest.

King David understood this. He often talked about the enjoyment and fulfillment that comes through knowing God, especially in the book of Psalms. Here's one example.

> *How precious is your unfailing love, O God!*
> *All humanity finds shelter*
> *in the shadow of your wings.*
> *You feed them from the abundance of your own house,*
> *letting them drink from your river of delights.*
> *For you are the fountain of life,*
> *the light by which we see.*
>
> (Psalm 36:7–9)

We enjoy life because we were meant to. It is a gift. And it came from the one who knows the most about enjoyment. The one who created happiness, fun, satisfaction, and fulfillment. What does that mean for us?

First, it means we can get rid of the notion that pleasure and happiness are somehow anti-spiritual. Sometimes people think that suffering makes us holier or more pleasing to God, but that isn't true. God created life to be enjoyed, and our happiness makes him happy. Yes, he uses suffering to our advantage. But that doesn't mean that he wants us to be in pain—it just proves that he's more powerful than our pain.

Second, we can enjoy God. We can relish following him and knowing him. We need to stop imagining God as a stressed-out, impossible-to-please dictator and start experiencing the joy, peace, and rest that he wants to give us.

Yes, I use this word a lot—but in this case it is completely justified. Life is *amazing*.

Questions for Reflection

- Do you enjoy life? What would help you enjoy it more?
- Is it hard for you to believe that God enjoys life or that he wants you to enjoy it as well? Why or why not?
- What are the top three most *amazing* things about the life God has given you?

32.

Just Wait

Bible Reading: 1 John 4:13-19

When I was a teenager, there were times I gave my mother some grief. I was a growing boy, testing my limits, and sometimes thought I could push her around a bit. Not literally, of course—I wouldn't be here today if I had ever done that. Let's be honest. I mean with my attitude. With my resistance to her authority.

"Son, I need you to clean your room," she would say.

"Aw, Mom. I don't really feel like it right now."

"I'm not asking if you feel like it. I'm telling you to do it."

"Well, um, I don't need to. It's pretty clean."

"Son—go clean your room. I'm not telling you again."

"No, I'm tired. I'll get to it later."

After a few rounds like that, my mom would stop arguing.

"Okay," she would say.

The first couple of times she did this I thought I had won. *Okay? Really?*

But she wasn't finished.

"Okay, Son. *Just wait until your dad gets home.*"

That became the most dreaded statement in my entire childhood. It was the phrase that sent chills up and down my spine. Instantly, I would lose all my cockiness and bravado. My pseudo-confidence would melt away, because I knew what would happen when Dad got home. This was not going to end well for me. My parents were firm believers in spankings.

"Mom, I totally apologize. I was just joking. You don't need to bother Dad. He's a pastor. He's busy helping people and building the church. Hey—have you lost weight?"

But she'd just smile casually as if to say, "Nice try, buddy, but it's too little, too late. Just wait until your dad gets home."

The house we lived in until I was twelve had a creaky, wooden front porch. My six-foot-three, 225-pound father made a particular kind of sound with his feet when he stepped on the porch. I remember listening for that sound. One agonizing hour would turn into two. Two hours would turn into three. Meanwhile, life held no charm. I couldn't enjoy my Atari. Watching *Saved by the Bell* wouldn't cheer me up. Nothing would fix the agony of anticipation.

When I heard the steps, I knew it was Dad. My moments were numbered. A few times I tried hiding, but that never worked out very well.

In retrospect, the most painful part about this whole thing wasn't when the leather hit my backside. It was the hours of anticipation leading up to that moment. The certainty that punishment was coming sucked the joy out of my life far more than the actual discipline.

I've noticed that sometimes we have a similar attitude of dread toward God. We view him as the great Judge and Defender of the universe. We think he carries a cosmic two by four, and he's scouring the earth, looking for miscreants who need a smackdown. So every time we make a mistake, we assume judgment is coming. Punishment is on its way. And since we're human and tend to make mistakes on a regular basis, we spend a lot of time listening for divine footsteps on the porch.

It's no wonder some of us don't enjoy God like we should. We're too busy hiding from him.

The Bible says that God disciplines those he loves, and he does it for our own benefit. So I'm not saying that we can do whatever we want and never worry about consequences. As people who love God, we want to live in a way that honors and pleases him.

What I'm saying is that we shouldn't live under the shadow of impending judgment. Even in his discipline, God is not an angry, vengeful specter of doom. He's not someone to dread or hide from. He's our father, and he loves us more than we could ever imagine.

God wants us to enjoy the life he has given us, but we

can't if we are always afraid the hammer is about to drop. He wants us to enjoy our relationship with him, but we won't, if we are scared that every time he shows up, his first order of business is punishment. John, one of Jesus' disciples, wrote this:

> This is how love is made complete among us so that we will have confidence on the day of judgment: In this world we are like Jesus. There is no fear in love. But perfect love drives out fear, because fear has to do with punishment. The one who fears is not made perfect in love. (1 John 4:17–18 NIV)

In other words, God doesn't want us to relate to him based on fear of punishment, but on love. Because of God's love, he sent Jesus to provide forgiveness of our sins. Because of God's love, we have confidence to approach him without fear of punishment.

This passage says, "In this world we are like Jesus." We have the righteousness, the acceptance, and the position with God that Jesus had. I can't imagine Jesus cowering in fear when God approaches. Quite the opposite. Jesus has complete confidence because he is loved by God and free from all sin.

That is how God sees us in Jesus. Free of sin. Cleared of guilt. Undeserving of punishment.

Don't let a wrong view of God steal the joy from your

existence. Learn to trust his love, and you will enjoy life with God as never before.

Questions for Reflection

- When you make a mistake, do you tend to think God is going to punish you for it? Is that correct? Why or why not?
- What is the purpose of God's discipline? How is this different from viewing God as an angry, judgmental disciplinarian?
- What does the phrase "In this world we are like Jesus" mean to you?

33.

Road Trip

Bible Reading: Psalm 139:7-10

What comes to mind when you hear the phrase "road trip"? The term conjures up different images for different people, I'm sure. But for most of us, the idea of hitting the open road, seeing new places, and enjoying great company is exciting.

The reality is not always so great, of course. For example, eating gets problematic. Fast food and road trips make a volatile combination. Many of us have found that out the hard way. And while we're on the topic, restrooms are rarely where you need them, when you need them most. But road trips are still fun. The spontaneity, the freedom, the break from your normal routine—it's great.

Until you have kids.

Now don't get me wrong. I love my kids. I just don't love being strapped into a speeding metal box, mere inches from my offspring, for hours on end. Something happens when kids and road trips collide. I think it's called reality.

The romance and the adventure are replaced by sibling squabbling and body odor. The long stretches behind the wheel turn into long waits at gag-inducing public restrooms because one child or another is always potty training and can't figure out how to do their thing on demand. The fascinating adult conversations are drowned out by VeggieTales and Disney songs—which I like, but not after three hours.

So when it comes to road trips, I've discovered something: it's all about whom you are with. The people in the other seats determine if your road trip is a comedy, a drama, or a horror flick.

When it comes to life, the same principle holds true. *Whom* you experience life with is usually far more important than *where* you live, *how much* money you have, *what* your occupation is, or many other things we tend to stress out about. Obviously the "whom" includes family and friends. But by far the most important person in your vehicle is—you guessed it— God. He is with you all the time, wherever you go. David wrote:

> *I can never escape from your Spirit!*
> *I can never get away from your presence!*
> *If I go up to heaven, you are there;*
> *if I go down to the grave, you are there.*
> *If I ride the wings of the morning,*
> *if I dwell by the farthest oceans,*

even there your hand will guide me,
and your strength will support me.

(Psalm 139:7–10)

We probably all agree that God is with us. We know he leads us, he protects us, and he loves us.

But . . . who gets to drive?

There used to be a bumper sticker that said, "God is my copilot." Then someone made one that said, "If God is your copilot, change seats." You can debate those two all you want, but I don't think they address the main point. Life isn't as much about control as it is about companionship. If we are in right relationship with God, we won't wrestle over the wheel. We'll travel together. We'll experience life together. Who drives? Who rides shotgun?

Most of the time it's a moot point. God is ultimately in charge, of course, but we get a lot of time at the wheel. Most likely, we'll take turns. We'll switch off, depending on the road ahead. And I think God wants it that way.

But here's the deal. Many times, we don't know our traveling companion as well as we think we do. We have a false view of who God is, and it affects how much we enjoy our journey. Here's my question. What is it like to journey with God? Whom do you think you are driving with?

Maybe you see God as a hitchhiker, a stranger you let into your car out of sheer grace. I've never picked up a hitchhiker. Sorry if that sounds prejudiced. I blame that on my mother—her warnings still ring in my ears. If you view God as a hitchhiker, even though you might have some interesting conversations, you'll never develop the relationship you should. He'll be a stranger, an interloper, someone who is here now and gone in a few hours.

Or maybe you see God as a backseat driver. I'm sure you've driven with a few of these. I'm about as far from this as possible, because most of the time, I'm looking at the guy driving, not the road—so I don't care how he drives. Do you view God as someone who is constantly harping on you and nagging at you? Who is second-guessing your decisions and telling you what you already know? If so, you'll tend to resent and resist his involvement in your life.

Or worst of all, maybe you see God as a driving-exam instructor. Remember when you first attempted to get your license? That day scarred many of us for life. There was no talking or joking or relationship. Just monosyllabic instructions and a lot of mysterious writing. Every mistake was written down in a book, and ultimately we passed or failed depending on our performance.

If that's how you view God, you'll think he is critiquing every move. He's recording every error and swerve. He's still making up his mind about whether to let you pass.

I hope you can see the error in each of those views of God. He isn't a hitchhiker: he's been with you every moment of the trip. He isn't a backseat driver: he trusts you and he believes in you. And he certainly isn't an exam instructor:

in his mind, you passed a long time ago, and he has no interest in recording your mistakes for future reference.

So who is God?

He's a friend.

The kind of friend you can say anything to. The kind of friend you can say nothing to for hours on end and he doesn't feel like he has to break the silence. A friend who gets your humor. Who knows what to say when you share your heart. Who makes you laugh loudly and think deeply and like yourself for who you are.

When you truly come to know God, the journey changes. The views are more spectacular. The drop-offs are less frightening.

And the road trip is fun again.

Questions for Reflection

- What is your relationship with God? To you, is he a hitchhiker, a backseat driver, an exam instructor—or a friend? What does that look like in your life?
- Is it hard for you to let God be involved in every detail of your journey? Why or why not?
- Who is more in control in your life—you or God? How do you know? Is it working well, or do either of you need to be more actively involved?

34.

The Secret of Living

Bible Reading: Philippians 4:10-19

I'm pretty sure that a hundred years from now, sociologists are going to look back at how much time we spend on our phones and wonder how the human race ever survived. Most of the time, of course, we don't talk on our phones. Who does that anymore? We look at them. We tap and type and swipe and scroll on them. We play bird-themed games and take endless pictures with them.

I love my phone. Too much, according to Chelsea. By nature I am both social and easily distracted, so having all that potential entertainment and interaction in the palm of my hand is like candy for my brain. But I have a problem with my phone. Specifically, with social media on my phone.

It's called FOMO. *Fear Of Missing Out.*

Maybe you've heard of it. Maybe you've even experienced it.

You can be happy and content with life. But then you open one of your eighty-seven social media apps, and suddenly you realize that some of your friends are at the beach. And not just any beach. It's a sunny, tropical, white-sand, blue-water, exotic beach. They are getting a tan and drinking something colorful with umbrellas in it.

Meanwhile, you are stuck at your desk. With a head cold. And deadlines and bad coffee and grumpy coworkers. And the weather outside is gray, cold, and wet. You know you should be happy for them. You know you've posted pictures of your vacations for others to drool over too. But you can't get over the fact that they are doing this *without you.*

I'm the worst at this particular malady, this social illness. I flip through Instagram for thirty seconds and see images of various buddies of mine skiing, tanning, preaching, working out, eating out, hanging out—and I find myself wishing I was doing every single one of those things with every single one of them right now. Simultaneously. What is wrong with me?

In my case, the solution was relatively easy. I deleted a bunch of apps from my phone. Problem (mostly) solved. I still engage with social media, but it's not my default, knee-jerk reaction anymore. It's something I do intentionally and for a limited time.

I hate to admit it, but the difference has been phenomenal.

I have more time and headspace to think and enjoy life. I engage with human beings in my vicinity rather than strangers around the world. I don't ignore my wife as often—that's really important, just FYI. And I am way more content, because I simply don't know what I'm missing out on.

By the way, this is not the solution for everyone. I understand that. Social media is an effective, healthy way for many people to stay in touch. So don't rush off and purge your phone just yet.

Mobile phones aside, I think that in general, many of us struggle with being content with where we are and even with who we are. We look at the talents and opportunities and lifestyles of others and we wish we could have what they have. Then we relegate our happiness to the distant future. We hope that someday we can have what they have, and then we will be happy. But if we can't be happy now, we won't be happy then. If we can't be content with what we have now, we won't be content in the future.

Vacationing in Maui is awesome, but it won't fill the void in our hearts. Playing golf for days on end sounds amazing, but it can't bring lasting happiness. Shopping sprees and fine dining and romantic dates and the public spotlight and hanging out with friends are all great—but they can't produce permanent peace.

On some level, we all probably agree with that. Especially when it comes to things like money, possessions, and fame. Those are famously shallow and short-lived. Things like relationships, marriage, and children are more fulfilling—but eventually they, too, prove incapable of providing sustainable satisfaction. The only thing that can bring us long-term contentment in life is relationship with God. He is the ultimate source of enjoyment and peace.

I don't mean to sound hyper-spiritual here. This is real. Far more real than your Instagram feed. God wants to live life with you. He wants to invade your day-to-day existence with his peace, his joy, and his purposes for you. And when he does, it changes everything.

The apostle Paul understood this. Despite some ridiculously depressing circumstances—things like multiple shipwrecks and prison sentences—his life was characterized by contentment and joy. He wrote this:

> I have learned how to be content with whatever I have. I know how to live on almost nothing or with everything. I have learned the secret of living in every situation, whether it is with a full stomach or empty, with plenty or little. For I can do everything through Christ, who gives me strength. (Philippians 4:11–13)

People often quote that last phrase about being able to do everything through Christ, but notice the context. It's talking specifically about being able to enjoy life. Jesus gives us the ability to be happy in any surroundings. That's quite a gift. Anyone can have fun lounging on a sun-swept beach. Anyone can be happy hanging out with best friends. But learning to find contentment through Jesus in any circumstance is what Paul called "the secret of living in every situation."

That's when life starts to really get good.

I can't promise you that following Jesus will make your FOMO fade forever. It's human nature to want to be where the party is, especially for particular personality types. But you can find contentment and joy in your current situation. No matter how ho-hum or humdrum or mundane that might be.

And once you find your fulfillment in God, you discover the secret of living.

Questions for Reflection

- Do you ever struggle with contentment? How do you respond when you are tempted to be jealous of someone else?
- How does knowing Jesus help you enjoy life even in potentially negative circumstances?
- Do you think contentment is "the secret of living in any situation"? Why or why not?

35.

The Struggle Is Real

Bible Reading: Matthew 11:28–30

I spend a lot of time thinking about what I wear. I'm not sure how normal this is for a guy, but I'm comfortable with it. Maybe it has to do with the fact that I spend an inordinate amount of time talking in front of crowds. As a pastor, conference speaker, and author, that's a large part of my job description. People have to look at me, so they might as well have something interesting to look at. I'm doing them a favor, right?

I like to keep people guessing about what I'm going to wear. If someone tells me they are glad I dress so progressively, I get nervous. I feel like I'm getting too predictable. So the next week I'll wear a suit. And if I get a compliment on how conservative I am, the next week I'll show up with the most avant garde outfit in my closet.

I blame my mom and my older sister for my obsession

with clothes and shopping. But it's who I am now, and I doubt I'm going to change. Shopping for me is less about wearing the clothing—although I clearly enjoy that part too—and more about the thrill of the hunt. The adrenaline of the chase. The excitement of finding the right color, texture, size, silhouette, season, and style. And then matching it with unexpected but completely rad accessories.

Then I get to the counter. And they ring up the bill. And I realize I have to tell Chelsea how much I just spent. It's what you'd call a reality check. And it's such a downer.

The struggle between doing what I love to do—shopping—and what I need to do—follow a budget—illustrates where we seem to spend a lot of our lives. We find ourselves caught between pleasure and practicality, between the glow of happiness and cold, hard reality. We feel like we need to balance what we want with what we need.

It's an either-or scenario: either we do what we want to do, or we do what we should do. But not both. The struggle is real. And let me be clear: in many cases, this struggle is not a bad thing. It's called maturity. Growing up. Self-control.

Part of being an adult is recognizing that working hard now brings more pleasure in the long run. It's the principle of delayed gratification. But I've noticed that sometimes we take this "work now, play later" principle to an extreme. When we do, we start to equate responsibility with toil and sacrifice, and irresponsibility with enjoyment and rest.

Similarly, when it comes to our walk with God, sometimes we assume that God's will for us is going to be hard, it's going to be painful, and it's going to cost us everything. Sometimes we think holiness means sacrifice and boredom, and sin means pleasure and freedom. But those stereotypes couldn't be further from the truth.

God designed life, after all. He came up with the concepts of fun and happiness and pleasure. It only makes sense that he would know best how to walk those paths, and that he would want to help us discover them.

Just because something is fun doesn't mean it is useless or wrong. And just because something is hard doesn't mean it is productive. That's a fallacy. Often, certain activities are fun and easy because they are *right*. We were designed to do them. It's a perfect fit. And many things that are hard and painful might feel that way because we were never meant to do them at all.

One of my favorite passages in the Bible is an invitation by Jesus to enjoy true life through him.

Then Jesus said, "Come to me, all of you who are weary and carry heavy burdens, and I will give you rest. Take my yoke upon you. Let me teach you, because I am humble and gentle at heart, and you will find rest for your souls. For my yoke is easy to bear, and the burden I give you is light." (Matthew 11:28–30)

I love the juxtaposition of work and rest, of burdens and ease. When we follow God, he doesn't remove our responsibilities. We don't take a permanent vacation from all activity. Rather, God makes our lives enjoyable. He makes them easy and light and fun. When we discover who God is, and when we allow him to lead our lives, we discover satisfaction and fulfillment as never before. We find why we were created and what we were designed to be good at.

Chances are, you are right where God wants you. You are doing what he wants you to do. You are becoming who he wants you to become. But maybe you need to be reminded that he also wants you to enjoy life. You don't have to choose between having fun and having a future. Between pragmatism and pleasure. They aren't mutually exclusive. In the middle of your daily responsibilities and challenges, God wants to give you a new level of joy.

Or maybe you do need to make a few changes in your life. Maybe the fact that you enjoy certain things or are gifted at them is a hint that God wants to move you in that direction.

Either way, don't give up on enjoying life in the name of holiness, productivity, or responsibility. God is big enough and good enough to lead you down paths that are both productive and satisfying.

Questions for Reflection

- What are some things you enjoy doing and are good at? How do you feel when you do the things you are gifted at?
- Are there areas of your life that God wants you to enjoy more? What are some ways you could enjoy them?
- Have you ever heard people say that being a Christian is boring or hard work? Are they right? Why or why not?

36.

Bedtime Stories

Bible Reading: Numbers 6:24–26

Putting small children to bed is not all that it's sometimes portrayed to be. If you're a parent, you know what I mean. Before I had kids, I thought bedtime would be this tranquil, laughter-filled bonding time between parents and kids. I imagined myself reading stories to my darling, pajama-clad cherubs as they snuggled up next to me. In my fantasy, these adorable beings would then crawl gratefully into bed; I would kiss them goodnight; and they would silently sink into peaceful slumber. Then I would go downstairs and mess around with their mother all evening.

Parents, let's be honest. The reality is not quite so picturesque. It's less Mary Poppins and more Stephen King. Bedtime is laborious. It's painful. It's scarring. It's a drawn-out process that usually involves commands, threats, pleas, manipulation, bribery, and sheer physical force.

The drama begins when you announce that bedtime is upon them. "Kids, it's time for bed." But they don't hear those words. What they hear is, "Kids, it's time to die." So they react with wails and shrieks and emotional pleas to be granted five more minutes of life on this planet. When they realize begging for mercy is futile, the next stage of their resistance kicks in.

Instant lethargy.

They are stricken with a sudden inability to navigate stairs or clutch a toothbrush or pull back covers. "Dad, I need someone to help meeeeeeeee."

Once you get past that stage, and you get them under the covers, and you pray with them, and you kiss them—you've only just begun. Guaranteed, every kid will have last requests.

"I need a different pillow."

"Scratch my back."

"Tell my brother to be quiet."

"Leave the door open a crack. More than that. More, more . . . No, not that much."

"Open the window."

"Close the window."

And then you kiss them goodnight. Again. You go find your spouse, who by this time has fallen asleep on the couch. But you're too exhausted and emotionally drained to be romantic, so you settle for watching reruns of *The Office*.

Then five minutes into your show, when you are just start-ing to relax and forget your trauma, a voice comes wafting down the stairs.

"Dad, I need a drink of water—"

But eventually their resistance gives way to the force of nature, and they fall silent. It's not some slow, angelic transition, either. There is no drifting or sinking or sailing slowly into slumber. One second they are yelling or laughing or jumping on their beds or pummeling each other, and then *wham*! Utter silence.

The quiet is more disconcerting than the noise, though. Are they asleep? Or are they plotting revenge? So you go upstairs to make sure they are okay. You find them sound asleep. And as you look at their faces, your heart melts. Instantly the trauma of bedtime, the stress of your day, and the worries of life fall into their rightful and secondary place. You feel nothing but love and joy and gratitude for the beings before you.

Your kids aren't doing a thing to earn your approval. They are sound asleep. If anything, you should be a little upset because they fought so hard. And because they messed up your amorous intentions. But you aren't upset. You simply revel in the fact that they are yours. That you get to spend the rest of your life knowing them, loving them, and being loved by them.

At that moment, you get a glimpse of what God feels for you and me. You start to realize the sheer enjoyment and pleasure that he must feel when he looks down at his children.

God reveals his father's heart of love throughout the Bible. One of the most beautiful instances is found in the book of Numbers. This passage is a prayer of blessing that God told the priests to pray over the people.

> *May the LORD bless you*
> *and protect you.*
> *May the LORD smile on you*
> *and be gracious to you.*
> *May the LORD show you his favor*
> *and give you his peace.*
> (Numbers 6:24–26)

Why did God command them to pray this way? Because he wanted to answer their prayers. This is a description of his nature. It is his default attitude and approach toward us.

God enjoys us. He smiles when he sees us. He pours out his blessings and grace and favor upon us. He delights in the simple reality that we are his and we get to be together forever. God's relationship with us is not born out of duty, or desire for control, or obsession with performance.

Sometimes I think we look at God like some frazzled, frustrated, overworked dad who just wants us to leave him alone so he can get back to what is really important to him. We assume he wishes we'd shape up and shut up so his job would be easier.

I've got news for you. *We* are what is important to him. *We* are his job, his priority, his obsession. There is nothing more pressing to God than relationship with his children. The entire plan of redemption revolves around God's goal to bring us back into fellowship with him.

Yes, as God's kids, we tend to overreact a lot. We complain and disobey and whine sometimes. But God isn't up in heaven rolling his eyes or raising his voice. He isn't telling the angels, "I can't do this. It's your turn. You go get him the drink of water."

He's our father, and he loves us. He smiles at us. He forgives us quickly and completely. He dreams about our futures. He looks forward to us waking up in the morning so he can spend time with us.

He loves to be with us—when we are at our best, and when we are at our worst.

God enjoys us.

And that means we can enjoy him.

Questions for Reflection

- Do you ever wonder if God is irritated with your neediness or weakness? Why or why not?
- How would you describe God's attitude and feelings toward you as his child?
- Why does the fact that God enjoys us mean that we can enjoy him?

37.

I Don't Know

Bible Reading: Romans 12:3–21

When you are a student, life revolves around knowing *answers*. Tests, for example, are a series of questions and answers. Homework is about writing down the right answers. If you get called on in class, you had better know the answer the teacher is looking for. It's all about what you know. If you don't know the answers, you fail. You don't measure up. You are rejected.

Maybe that's why school wasn't easy for me. The social side of school was great—I loved that. If there had been classes called Talking or Joke-Telling or Wasting Time Loudly, I would have passed those with straight As. But unfortunately, that wasn't the case. My classes were things like British Literature and Biology and Pre-Algebra. And in those classes they required you to learn things. To acquire knowledge and facts and information. It was so unfair.

As a defense mechanism, I got really good at making stuff up. That is a God-given talent of mine. And I honed and shaped it to perfection. I might not have learned the principal exports of Kazakhstan or the names of all the planets (good thing, because Pluto got kicked out of the club anyway), but I learned how to come up with answers that sounded awesome, even though they had no basis in reality. I did whatever it took to avoid that phrase of death: "I don't know."

Then high school ended and life began. As I've gotten older, I've discovered a surprising and liberating reality: *you don't have to know all the answers.*

Maybe that's not a surprise to you. Maybe you have absolutely no problem saying "I don't know." You are the first to admit when you are lost. You are the person who immediately asks for directions. You read instruction manuals. Maybe you are so secure in who you are that your deficiencies and weaknesses don't bother you.

Most of us are not like that. At least not by nature. The human tendency is to project a persona that says, *I am in control. I know what I'm doing and where I'm going. And I don't need help from anyone.*

When I was a youth pastor, it was fairly easy to feel in control, to think that I was enough for the task at hand. I could tell the young people anything and they'd believe me.

I was older, I was married, I had a kid or two at the time—so I was the expert at life. It was awesome.

But then I started preaching in the adult service. And I realized very quickly that I was not smart enough, experienced enough, or mature enough to be everybody's answer man. The thought that they might expect that scared me to death.

After all, I was addressing successful businesspeople who had made millions by the time they were my age. I was teaching couples who had grandchildren older than I was. I was preaching to people who knew the Bible better, who had experienced more in life than I had, and who were in many ways more qualified than I was. And here's what I learned: *that's okay.* I'm not the answer for people anyway. Jesus is.

God didn't call me because I knew everything. He didn't give me influence because I'm better than everyone else. He called me because it was his good pleasure to use me to help people. Even with my weaknesses and deficiencies.

Maybe you live under the impression that you have to have it all together. That any sign of weakness will be pounced upon and used against you. That you have to know all the answers.

You don't.

And you couldn't even if you tried. You might know a lot of the answers, and you should do your best to grow and improve and gain wisdom—but at the end of the day, you and

I are only human. We need God, and we need each other, and that's a good thing.

Here's something even better. Our lacks and weaknesses often open more doors than our talents and knowledge. Doors of relationship, of friendship, of intimacy. Doors of true growth and learning. There is something about admitting our needs that disarms even the most defensive people. It allows us to share ideas on an authentic and truly profound level.

Here are two great answers when we don't know the answer to a question:

I don't know. But I'll find out.

I don't know. What do you think?

Either of those is far better than making something up to protect our reputations as the answer men. No one is fooled by that anyway. If anything, people are turned off by it. They instinctively know not to trust someone who acts like they know everything.

The apostle Paul had a lot to say about recognizing our need for one another. He told the Roman church:

> Don't think you are better than you really are. Be honest in your evaluation of yourselves, measuring yourselves by the faith God has given us . . . Live in harmony with each other. Don't be too proud to enjoy the company of ordinary people. And don't think you know it all! (Romans 12:3, 16)

One of the secrets to enjoying life is to know what you know and to know what you don't know. That's more sustainable and enjoyable—and less exhausting—than trying to be everything for everyone all the time. Only God can be that. And the great thing is, we know God. We know who Jesus is. And ultimately, *who* we know is way more important than *what* we know anyway.

Our relationship with God gives us a confidence and joy that information—or speculation—could never provide.

Questions for Reflection

- Do you ever feel tempted to act like you know more than you do? Why or why not?
- What benefits have you experienced as a result of being vulnerable and humble about your weaknesses? How do people tend to respond to your honesty?
- Why is knowing Jesus more important than knowing data and information?

38.

Multitasking Times Infinity

Bible Reading: Matthew 10:29–31

I am not a multitasker. I am perhaps the furthest thing there has ever been from a multitasker, actually. So when I focus on someone, that person has my full and undivided attention. Only for about thirty seconds, though, because I am also easily distracted. It's a terrible combination. I need professional help.

In case we ever meet in person, and I randomly interrupt our conversation to comment about an odd bird on a branch or the awesome outfit you are wearing, let me just say—it's not you. It's me.

The worst part about this particular combination of traits is the effect it has on my driving habits. I should probably not be allowed on the road without blinders, the kind that horses wear in parades. Sure, that might mess with my peripheral vision, but it would be preferable to the state of distraction that defines my driving.

My dad used to send me to pick up friends at the airport. As I drove them back to the house or the church, we would always become engaged in some riveting conversation. Inevitably I would forget that I was the driver, and I would turn my full attention—and gaze—to the speaker. Eye contact is important, I was taught.

I would notice my passengers' eyes getting wider. Occasionally they would gasp or twitch violently. I'm sure pedestrians were diving out of crosswalks and bicycles were swerving into trashcans on the sidewalk. But I was oblivious. Sooner or later, my captive audiences would either end the conversation or offer to drive the rest of the way. And who could blame them? They feared for their lives.

If I am the worst multitasker ever, God is the best. He simultaneously coordinates the cares, concerns, prayers, needs, decisions, and existence of billions of people. And he's not stressed about it, nor is he running anyone off the road. He is able to concentrate completely on you and me without losing focus on anyone else. Jesus said this about God's focus and attention span:

> What is the price of two sparrows—one copper coin? But not a single sparrow can fall to the ground without your Father knowing it. And the very hairs on your head are all

numbered. So don't be afraid; you are more valuable to God than a whole flock of sparrows. (Matthew 10:29–31)

Sometimes our lifestyles and prayers make it seem as if we don't believe that. Let me explain.

I've heard people say that we shouldn't pray for our basketball team to win, for example. Or for short lines when we renew our driver's licenses. Or for parking spots on Christmas Eve. In comparison to the things God must have on his mind, these people reason, those requests are petty and selfish. We should save our prayers for things that really matter.

First of all, finding a spot on Christmas Eve is not a "small" request. It's a greater miracle than walking on water, in my opinion. Have you ever tried it?

But more than that, this sort of comment reveals that we don't think God cares about the details of our existence. Yes, we believe he holds the universe in his hands. He is architecting the future of humanity. He is planning how to reach the unsaved people groups of the world, how to help victims of disasters and plagues, how to build a church that influences society, and how to fix our weaknesses and sins. He is focused on those things. He is concentrating on his grand plans and dreams. Why would he care about my little needs? My petty preferences and ridiculous requests?

But that reasoning is wrong. It is the result of taking our finite, limited abilities and superimposing them on God.

God is not an either-or God. He doesn't answer one prayer or supply one need at the expense of another. He doesn't have to choose between you and me. He doesn't have a limited amount of time or attention or resources. He's infinite. He is capable of caring about the greatest tragedies and the tiniest inconveniences at the same time. He is able to laugh with those who laugh while he weeps with those who weep.

We can't, of course. We either drive or talk. We either laugh or cry. We are focused on our details, our existence, and our reality. It's the nature of being human. We can only care about so much.

God wants to expand our spheres, of course. He wants to help us see beyond our needs. So I'm not advocating selfishness here. Rather, I'm talking about believing in a God who is big enough to take care of us and also take care of the world. I'm talking about being bold enough and confident enough in God's love to believe that he wants us to enjoy life and he will allocate resources to help that happen.

This understanding frees us to love the world around us more because we know the details of our own existence are safely held in God's hand. And it gives us even greater faith to believe for world change, because we know that we serve a limitless God.

Just because God has a lot on his mind doesn't mean he cares for you any less. And just because he provides for you doesn't mean he's ignoring the needs of the world around you.

He's big enough and good enough for both.

Questions for Reflection

- Do you ever feel like your needs and prayers are a bother to God? Why or why not?
- How would you describe the level of interest God takes in your life? Why is it sometimes hard to believe he cares so much?
- How does trusting in an infinite God give us faith for both our own problems and world-sized problems?

39

Look at the View

Bible Reading: Psalm 103:1–12

I enjoy interior design. I like thinking about spaces and trying to create a particular mood. But one of the problems with being the interior designer for your own home is that you develop blind spots. You are too close to the project, so you stop noticing things after a while. For example, maybe you installed white carpet despite having three small children. Really? Who would do that?

I would.

So you make your kids and spouse and guests take off their shoes upon entry. That's great in theory, but the inevitable result is a pile of abandoned shoes stacking up just inside your front door. You don't even recognize all the shoes anymore. Apparently some of your guests left in their socks at some point. Each day when you come home the door is harder to open, and you have to shimmy past a Mount Everest of footwear to get through. But you don't stop to think about it, because you don't even see them anymore.

Or you have one blank wall in your house that is crying out for some sort of decoration or accessory, so you buy an awesome picture for it. But you don't have time to hang the picture just then, because that would involve hammers and nails and other home improvement things you subconsciously avoid. So for now you lean it up against the wall.

And there it sits—for days. And weeks. And months. Every time you vacuum you have to move it, but when you're done, you move it right back to its customary spot against the wall. Then one day one of your friends comes over, and he's like, "Hey, so . . . I can hang that for you, if you'd like." Suddenly you realize how odd and unfinished it looks to everyone else. You just didn't notice it anymore.

On the other hand, we can also get immune to the beautiful things around us. Maybe you buy a house with a spectacular view. That view cost you more than you'd like to admit. But when you first saw it, you could imagine yourself out on the deck every morning, sipping coffee, and just meditating on how good life is—so you bought the house with the view.

But after a month or two, you don't see the view anymore. You drink your coffee in the car like you always used to because you got up late and have to rush out the door. Then someone comes to visit and she says, "Wow, it must be so incredible to wake up to a view like that every day."

And you look at it and you're like, "Um, yes it is. I guess. I had forgotten about that."

The old cliché "Familiarity breeds contempt" is probably true sometimes, but I think more often than not, familiarity breeds indifference. Or dare I say, even ingratitude. It seems like it's human nature to become oblivious to the things we see every day. It's normal and natural—almost inevitable—to take things for granted, to overlook the obvious.

When that indifference is directed at our home decorating or the view from our living room window, it's not a big deal. But here's what concerns me. As Jesus followers, sometimes we do the same thing with the good news of God's salvation. We've heard so much about God's love and grace that sometimes we start to tune it out. Instead of good news, it becomes old news. And that's a problem.

Then we meet someone who just started following Jesus. And they are like, "Man, did you realize that Jesus died for us? That God loves us? That he takes care of us and accepts us and helps us? This is amazing! This is incredible! I've been looking for this my whole life!"

And we respond, "Um, yeah—I guess I had forgotten about that."

I'm not trying to put a guilt trip on any of us. This isn't about artificially reciting our blessings just so we can be grateful people. It's about taking a fresh look at the unimaginably awesome gifts of God, at the things that surround us so consistently that sometimes we forget they are there. It's about being genuinely and continually amazed by God. By the simple truths of the gospel. By the reality of his love and grace. King David wrote this:

> *Let all that I am praise the Lord;*
>> *may I never forget the good things he does for me.*
> *He forgives all my sins*
>> *and heals all my diseases.*
> *He redeems me from death*
>> *and crowns me with love and tender mercies.*
> *He fills my life with good things.*
>> *My youth is renewed like the eagle's!*
>
> (Psalm 103:2–5)

Sometimes, quite simply, we forget what we have. We don't mean to. It's just that life gets busy, worries creep in, and deadlines take over. And days or weeks or months pass without us ever really engaging in the goodness of God.

When we realize our relationship with God feels a bit routine, often we think the answer to our apathy is to discover more complex, profound things about God. The basic, simple things like God's grace and love seem almost elementary. Those are for newbies in the faith. For novices.

We think that if we can learn new things about God, if we can get past the milk of the gospel and get to the meat, we will enjoy God more. So we get enamored with questions about the end times, and about prophecies and spiritual gifts, and about debates over whether alcohol is sin and if Santa Claus is the devil. But Jesus' death and resurrection aren't basic. They aren't an introduction to the real gospel.

They *are* the gospel.

Growing in knowledge has its place, of course. And doctrinal purity and biblical study are essential. As a pastor, that's a large part of my job. But the more I study the Bible, the more I discover something. The good news of God's forgiveness is both simple and profound. God's love is clear enough for a child to grasp, but it's complex enough that we will spend the rest of our lives trying to understand it—and we never fully will.

But the key to enjoying life isn't learning new doctrines and theology. And it isn't found in the minutiae and the complexities of religion.

It's found in rediscovering the simplicity right in front of us.

Questions for Reflection

- Do you ever find yourself forgetting the good things God has done for you? Why or why not?
- What are the truths about God that have changed your life the most? Are they simple or complex?
- How does focusing on Jesus and the gospel help you enjoy God more?

40.

The Most Important Thing

Bible Reading: Luke 10:38-42

I've noticed a particular cultural phenomenon. I don't know if it's specifically American, but we have definitely embraced it wholeheartedly. It's our fascination with being busy. Our culture is enamored and enthralled with busyness. Have you noticed? We are addicted to it. We walk fast, we talk fast, we eat fast, we entertain ourselves fast, and we work fast.

We measure our worth with a simple formula: how much we get done divided by how long it took. I just referenced math, in case you didn't notice. That's a big deal for me. Anyway, busyness permeates and dominates our society. Even our clichés illustrate this. *Busy as a beaver. Busy as a bee. Busy as a bear in a beehive.* Apparently our clichés also happen to all be animal-related. Not sure what that means.

Busy people, we assume, get more done. And that means they are important. They are significant. They live life to the fullest. So we take on more and more responsibility. We multitask everything. We chain-drink double espressos with a couple of chocolate-covered coffee beans on the side. We live life on fast-forward because it feeds our sense of value. Then, exhausted, we fall into bed at night and wonder why we feel stressed. And sometimes even a little empty.

I'm certainly not knocking productivity or hard work. But sometimes in the name of efficiency, busyness can become an end in itself, rather than a means to an end. We can end up measuring our worth by our work and our significance by our stress level.

One thing I appreciate about my dad was his refusal to be a busy dad. In retrospect, I realize he carried tremendous responsibility. Throughout my childhood and teen years, there was a never-ending demand upon his time, energy, and focus. Yes, there were seasons when the schedule was crazy, the workload was too much, and emotions were stretched thin. But for my dad, that was the exception, not the expectation.

I don't remember him being a busy or stressed-out person. And as his son, that was incredibly affirming. I knew he had time for me. I knew he had energy for me. I knew he enjoyed being with me. Even with the demands and distractions of growing up in a pastor's home, life was enjoyable. God was fun.

Now that I find myself in his role, I appreciate more than ever his ability to relax and make life fun. In some ways, my burden is not even close to what his was. Yet sometimes when my kids ask me to play, I find myself shooing them away. Not so much because I have a pressing deadline, but because playing seems so . . . unproductive.

"Not now kids. I have to study. I have to work. I have to serve God, and it's hard work, and it's tedious and terrible, but somebody has to do it."

That's a slight exaggeration. But you get the picture.

Busyness is not as much a schedule as it is an attitude and an approach toward life. We can work hard and not be busy. And we can be busy and not really be that effective. Sometimes rest is the most productive thing we can do. Sometimes slowing down can have better results than stressing, straining, and striving.

It's funny. We admire busyness, but when it comes down to it, we aren't attracted to busy people. We don't want to be raised by busy parents. We don't want to be pastored by a busy pastor. We don't want to hang out with busy friends. There's something about busyness that tends to torpedo relationships, which in the long run bring far more satisfaction than just getting stuff done.

It's worth noting that Jesus wasn't characterized by busyness. He lived a lifestyle of rest, joy, and peace. Even though he worked hard and went through tough times, he knew how to enjoy life with God. One time he was at the house of some of his best friends—Mary, Martha, and Lazarus. Martha was busy working, but Mary was just sitting with Jesus, listening to him. That made Martha mad, so she complained to Jesus. Martha expected him to call Mary out—but he did the opposite.

But Martha was distracted with much serving, and she approached Him and said, "Lord, do You not care that my sister has left me to serve alone? Therefore tell her to help me."

And Jesus answered and said to her, "Martha, Martha, you are worried and troubled about many things. But one thing is needed, and Mary has chosen that good part, which will not be taken away from her." (Luke 10:40–42 NKJV)

It's a bit ironic: Martha thinks Mary is distracted from what's important. But Martha is the distracted one. Because she is working so hard, she is missing out on the most important thing—relationship with Jesus.

The way to avoid busyness is not to work less. It's not to default on the rest of life in the name of relationship and peace. That's not what Jesus was saying here. The way to avoid busyness is to focus on Jesus. It's to learn to be loved by him and to love him. And after that, it's to value relationships with others.

Responsibilities, pressures, and deadlines are part of life. But they don't have to be the *point* of life. As we learn to live in love, peace, faith, and joy, even the busy bits of life become more satisfying and fulfilling. Ultimately, Jesus is the focus of who we are and what we do. Don't let the chaos and craziness of life distract you from him. That's the point of this devotional and the *Life Is* _____ book.

Be loved by him and love him.
Trust him in every moment.

Be at peace with him and with yourself.

Enjoy him.

Those are simple things. Anyone can do them, and all of us should. But they aren't necessarily second nature, especially in a busy world. They take humility, intentionality, and practice. But the result is worth it. When God is at the center of your world, everything changes.

Jesus makes life make sense.

He makes your existence fun again.

Questions for Reflection

- What are the "busy" things that distract you from relationship with God and others in your life? How can you rest more even in the middle of your many responsibilities?
- Do you tend to find your value in what you do or in who you are in Jesus? Why?
- During the last forty days, what things have you learned that have most impacted your life?
- Moving forward, how can you keep Jesus at the center of your day-to-day life? What are some ways you could become more focused on Jesus than on yourself?

About the Author

Judah and Chelsea Smith are the lead pastors of the City Church based in Seattle, Washington. Judah is a well-known speaker at conferences and churches around the world. His humorous yet poignant messages demystify the Bible and show people who Jesus is in their everyday lives. Judah is the author of the *New York Times* bestseller *Jesus Is _____*. Before assuming the lead pastorate in 2009, Judah led the youth ministry of the City Church for ten years. He has authored several books and is a popular voice on Twitter (@judahsmith). Judah and Chelsea have three children: Zion, Eliott, and Grace. Judah is an avid golfer and all-around sports fan. He believes the Seahawks are God's favorite team and is praying for the Sonics to come back to Seattle.